SALVATION STORY

Salvationist Handbook of Doctrine

SALVATION STORY

Salvationist Handbook
of Doctrine

The Salvation Army International Headquarters
London, England

First Published 1998
COPYRIGHT © 1998 THE GENERAL OF THE SALVATION ARMY
ISBN 085412 659 7 (cloth)
ISBN 085412 660 0 (paper)
Second edition 1999
ISBN 085412 678 3

GENERAL ORDER

This volume contains an exposition of the principal Doctrines of The Salvation Army as set forth in its Deed Poll of 1878 and confirmed in The Salvation Army Act 1980. It is for the use of all Salvationists.

These Doctrines are to be taught in connection with all Salvation Army officers' training operations, both preparatory and institutional.

It is required of officers of all ranks that their teaching, in public and private, shall conform to these eleven Articles of Faith.

International Headquarters
LONDON, England

Scripture quotations from the *New International Version* Copyright © 1986 by the International Bible Society

Cover design by Mickhail Gavrilov
Produced by UK Territory Print and Design Unit
Printed and bound in Great Britain by
MPG Books Ltd, Bodmin, Cornwall

TABLE OF CONTENTS

SALVATION ARMY DOCTRINES

As set out in Schedule 1 of The Salvation Army Act 1980

We believe that the Scriptures of the Old and New Testaments were given by inspiration of God, and that they only constitute the Divine rule of Christian faith and practice.

We believe that there is only one God, who is infinitely perfect, the Creator, Preserver, and Governor of all things, and who is the only proper object of religious worship.

We believe that there are three persons in the Godhead – the Father, the Son and the Holy Ghost, undivided in essence and co-equal in power and glory.

We believe that in the person of Jesus Christ the Divine and human natures are united, so that He is truly and properly God and truly and properly man.

We believe that our first parents were created in a state of innocency, but by their disobedience they lost their purity and happiness, and that in consequence of their fall all men have become sinners, totally depraved, and as such are justly exposed to the wrath of God.

We believe that the Lord Jesus Christ has by His suffering and death made an atonement for the whole world so that whosoever will may be saved.

We believe that repentance towards God, faith in our Lord Jesus Christ, and regeneration by the Holy Spirit, are necessary to salvation.

We believe that we are justified by grace through faith in our Lord Jesus Christ and that he that believeth hath the witness in himself.

We believe that continuance in a state of salvation depends upon continued obedient faith in Christ.

We believe that it is the privilege of all believers to be wholly sanctified, and that their whole spirit and soul and body may be preserved blameless unto the coming of our Lord Jesus Christ.

We believe in the immortality of the soul; in the resurrection of the body; in the general judgment at the end of the world; in the eternal happiness of the righteous; and in the endless punishment of the wicked.

FOREWORD

What Salvationists believe has never been incidental to how we live out our life in Christ as individuals, or as a global spiritual movement. Our faith, grounded in Scripture, and validated victoriously by personal experience, has been the motive force of our obedience in mission. *Salvation Story* is written to assist us in reflecting on the foundation of that faith, and its meaning for our life together as the people of God in mission and for our programmes of redemptive and compassionate action.

It is an important step forward in better understanding ourselves and what our statement of faith commits us to in the light of the word of God. *Salvation Story* puts us all into the flow of what God has been doing across the centuries for the salvation of the world. It is our story. For we believe that God raised up The Salvation Army as part of his programme, born of love from all eternity, to heal and restore a broken humanity and draw it back into fellowship with himself.

These chapters not only aid our understanding of our eleven doctrines that form the basis of belief for our evangelical mission, they draw out the contemporary relevance of these doctrinal statements and relate them effectively to our experience and calling as Salvationists today.

The vital heart of the faith of Salvationists is the redeeming blood of Christ and the purifying and empowering fire of the Spirit. We are an army of 'Blood and Fire'. But now other words like 'community', 'mission', 'sacramental', and 'church', are more important to our story than ever. They help us to understand what our new life in Christ makes possible and necessary for sustaining our inner life, fighting the good fight of faith and fulfilling our role in the grand scheme of human redemption.

General Eva Burrows gave a mandate to the International Doctrine Council in 1992 to prepare a new Handbook of Doctrine with a fresh approach. *Salvation Story* is the fulfilment of that charge. During the whole of the project, the original council has remained intact with the exception of changes in its chairman and secretary. Every Salvationist is indebted to them, and to the corresponding members, for their prayerful participation in the preparation of *Salvation Story*.

David Guy, Chairman	Gudrun Lydholm
Earl Robinson, Chairman	Christine Parkin
John Amoah	Rae Major, Secretary
Phil Needham	Benita Robinson, Secretary
Raymond Caddy	

Salvation Story is issued with the prayer that it will be a means of grace to all Salvationists who study its pages and that, by the power of the Spirit, its illumination of the essentials of our faith will be translated into saving action.

General Paul A. Rader
International Headquarters
London, England

INTRODUCTION

This book is about the faith of the Salvationist. It is based upon the eleven Articles of Faith which, since 1878, have been the basis of The Salvation Army's witness to the Christian gospel.

Some may wonder why Salvationists place such emphasis upon a written statement of faith. After all, they are people who rightly maintain that a Christian is one who enters trustfully into a relationship with the Lord Jesus Christ and is born again of the Holy Spirit. They emphasise that faith is a personal affair, often springing from an experience of God's grace that is beyond the reach of definition or analysis. They may well be suspicious of any attempt to reduce this life-changing encounter to a form of words on a page.

Yet without words, the experience fails to be named, clarified or shared. Faith is not only personal: it has a public face. The earliest Christians acknowledged one another in the simple confession: 'Jesus is Lord' (1 Corinthians 12:3). This was their creed. As they shared it, they grounded their personal experience in the risen Christ, verified one another's experience and called upon the world to acknowledge the lordship of Christ. It was from these biblical beginnings that the creeds of the Church grew to be authoritative statements of the Christian faith. They have a long history, some of which is referred to within these pages.

Doctrine is the teaching of the Church. It is an expanded explanation of faith, founded on Scripture and developed from a basic creed. The eleven Articles of Faith are an expression both of personal faith and of a common vision.

They are consistent with the classical Christian creeds and identify Salvationists as members of the universal Church. They also express the fundamental evangelical convictions of Wesleyanism, the branch of the Church out of which The Salvation Army grew. Salvationists emphasise in their doctrine and in their mission the universal call to personal salvation, the challenge to holiness and the need for evangelical zeal.

The Eleven Doctrines have remained essentially unchanged in a rapidly changing world. A number of Handbooks of Doctrine have, however, been produced, the most recent of which was published in 1969. It was decided that the time was fitting for a further explanatory volume.

This book differs from its predecessors in a number of ways. It is narrative in form, so that teaching is presented in short paragraphs, rather than point by point. This should enable the progression of thought to be clearly seen and allow for flexible use in both study groups and the classroom. The narrative style means that we examine the truths of our faith on two levels, both as the work of God in history which accomplished our salvation, and as the record of our own journey of faith, from sin through to salvation and holiness. The narrative approach is reflected, too, in the Handbook's title: *Salvation Story.*

Salvationists base their understanding of doctrine on the witness of the Bible, the living word of God. Our Articles of Faith make that clear, and therefore this book seeks to be faithful to Scripture. Scripture references appear throughout and can usually be found at the end of the section to which they relate. References are selective rather than comprehensive and allow students to research those that are helpful and to discover others for themselves.

This Handbook is deliberately concise. Its purpose is to provide a testament to the faith that is shared by Salvationists all over the world. For that reason, it is written throughout in the first person plural. It is hoped that Salvationists will recognise within it a commonly understood approach to Christian truth and identify themselves with it. Furthermore, it is not intended to be exclusive to Salvationists. It allows them to declare what they believe and to invite others to share the same experience of saving grace.

This book, with its accompanying Study Guide and other publications, will provide a useful resource for all Salvationists, including new converts and officer-cadets, in their study of the fundamentals of our faith.

CHAPTER ONE

Word of the living God

The source of Christian doctrine

Related Doctrines

We believe that the Scriptures of the Old and New Testaments were given by inspiration of God, and that they only constitute the Divine rule of Christian faith and practice.

The source of Christian doctrine is the Bible. We hold a faith that finds its definition and defence in Scripture. For this reason, the First Article is a preliminary statement that establishes the Bible as the sourcebook for Christian doctrine.

The Bible is a book written by many writers: it is a human document. But we believe that it is also God's written word. It carries God's authority and it is also the revealer of truth and the guide for Christian living. In its pages we encounter the living God of history and we hear his voice. For this reason, we are people of the Book.

■ Matthew 19:3-6; Mark 12:26-27; John 5:37-47; Acts 17:1-3; 1 Thessalonians 2:13; 2 Timothy 3:16-17

1

A word in time

God's word has been given to us in the recorded experiences of men and women of faith over many centuries. The Bible is the fruit of a living relationship between God and his people in a particular historical context.

The Canon

The Canon is that body of literature accepted by the Church as Holy Scripture, the revealed word of God. It is comprised of both the Old and New Testaments. The first Christians accepted the Jewish sacred writings, the Old Testament, as authoritative and appealed to its content to support the claims they were making for the divine mission and authority of Jesus. At the same time, they began to communicate the gospel message by the written as well as the spoken word. Certain of these writings were recognised as possessing authority from very early in the Church's history. In the course of time they become our New Testament.

The Old Testament originated in the experience of the Jewish people over many centuries. It records the developing but still incomplete revelation of God prior to the coming of his Son, Jesus Christ. Christians have always loved and venerated the Old Testament while recognising that the true interpretation of its meaning and the fulfilment of its promise are found only in Jesus. This is the central message of the New Testament. Without the New, the Old Testament remains incomplete. Conversely, the New Testament is incomplete without the Old. What the New Testament announces is the fulfilment of the yearnings and hopes of the Old Testament in Jesus Christ.

The New Testament is the written testimony to the life, teaching and person of the Lord Jesus Christ. Its books were written to instruct believers and bring others to faith in Christ.

When the Canon was established in the fourth century, most of the books in our New Testament were universally acknowledged by the Christian community. Those about which some reservation was expressed were included or excluded on the basis of three guidelines: authentic books were to be of apostolic origin, conform to the accepted rule of faith, and be commonly used by the churches.

By this careful process, guided by the Holy Spirit, Christians reached a consensus about the books regarded as Scripture. In no case did a Church council attempt to declare a book canonical that had not already been broadly accepted by the Christian congregations. The authority of Scripture was not bestowed. It was recognised and, when recognised, affirmed.

Testaments

The 66 books which comprise the Bible are divided into Old and New Testaments, diverse writings united by a common theme. Testament means covenant. The Jewish Scriptures witness to the covenant established by God with Israel. The New Testament testifies to the new covenant established through Jesus Christ for all people, effective for all who trust in him.

These books, differing widely in literary form and cultural background, may be studied as individual expressions of historic cultures. Christians, however, regard them as one book – the Bible. There is one theme, the saving grace of God, and one story, God's dealing with his people, culminating in the saving work of God in Christ. There are two testaments and one revelation. Thus these writings stand alone as a unique witness and possess unique authority deriving from their content, theme and divine origin. (*See appendix 1.*)

■ **Exodus 31:18; 32:15-16; 2 Kings 22:8-10; 23:1-3; Nehemiah 8:1-8; Jeremiah 36:1-6; Habakkuk 2:2; Luke 1:1-4; 24:25-27, 44-48; John 20:30-31; Acts 1:1-2**

Revelation

All generations have witnessed to an awareness of divine presence, or to a conviction that the beauty and order of the universe suggest an almighty Creator. But unaided we can make little progress in any quest to discover the saving truth about God. This is partly because God must always remain essentially a mystery to his creation. And since our perceptions have been affected by sin, our understanding of God is clouded and distorted.

We believe that God, through his actions, has made known to us what we could never discover for ourselves – his loving character, saving power and eternal purpose. He has 'removed the veil' that shrouded his mystery. This self-revelation of God is faithfully preserved and presented in the living record of holy Scripture.

Revelation is a gift of grace, arising from God's love for humanity and the divine intention that we should come to know, love, serve and enjoy God for ever. The Bible is the record and written expression of that revelation. The insights of non-Christian religions may indicate spiritual awareness and understanding, but they do not present Jesus Christ as the Word made flesh.

The term revelation means to 'remove the veil'. In the Bible, revelation is seen to grow from the lesser to the greater and from the partial to the perfect. The self-revealing of God recorded in the Old Testament is gradual and necessarily partial, since it prepared the way for the coming of Christ, God's full and final revelation.

■ **Isaiah 55:8-11; John 1:14-18; Acts 14:17; Romans 1:18-20; 2:14-16; Galatians 1:11-12; 1 Peter 1:10-12**

Modes of revelation

God encounters human beings in many ways in the pages of Scripture. Through the events of their early history, the Jews were given a sense of the steadfast love of God. They recognised his hand in their formation as a people, and in their ongoing history. God gave the Law to provide a pattern for living in his company, and revealed the intensity and purity of his love through the prophets. In the Old Testament, history, law, prophecy and other writings contribute to a deepening understanding of God's majesty, holiness and love.

All of these various modes of revelation find their focus in Jesus Christ. God, active in history, acts uniquely in Jesus to bring his salvation. The one of whom the prophets spoke is also the fulfilment of the Law. The New Testament describes Jesus' personal history and proclaims the gospel message which the Church has preached ever since. So the Bible offers what no other book can offer in the same way – the word of Life. It is a saving revelation centred upon Jesus Christ, God's living Word.

■ **Psalm 96; 106; Isaiah 53:1-6; Hosea 11:1-4; Amos 5:21-24; Hebrews 1:1-3; 1 Peter 1:23-25**

Given by inspiration

Like the salvation to which it testifies, the Bible is God's gift not man's achievement. The Bible, too, results from the interplay of divine power and human response, God's enabling initiative and the free obedience of human agents. The precious treasure of revealed truth is communicated and preserved in the earthen vessel of written human language.

This miracle of divine grace is described in the term, 'divinely inspired', or 'given by inspiration of God'. The writers of the Bible, who often used many different literary sources, were so enlightened and directed by the Holy Spirit that they produced a wholly trustworthy and enduring witness to God's saving work for humanity, centred upon the life and person of Jesus Christ.

The writers enjoyed something more than the natural inspiration of an artist or author. At the same time, most Christians recognise that inspiration is not dictation, and there is nothing in Scripture to indicate that God obliterated the human personalities of the authors and turned them into copyists. Their own styles of writing, habits of thinking, cultural background and human limitations appear in the Bible's pages. Their thinking and writing were free and spontaneous, retaining style and individuality.

It is evident, however, that what resulted cannot be explained only in human terms. What the authors wrote was not their own work only, but also the work and word of God. An investigation into the message and claims of the Bible shows them to exceed conventional human wisdom, logic and goodness.

God's revelation does not originate with us. (*See appendix 2.*)

■ **Jeremiah 1:1-3; 1 Corinthians 2:12-13; 2 Timothy 3:14-17; 2 Peter 1:20-21**

Authority

Because the Bible is given by inspiration and contains the saving revelation of God, the authority of Scripture overshadows all other authority. The Jewish people accepted the authority of their sacred writings. Jesus concurred. Following the example of its Lord, the Early Church, from its inception, recognised and appealed to the Jewish Canon and saw in it the foundations of the gospel. However, it also came very quickly to recognise the inspiration and authority of writings which together came to form the New Testament. These writings are also foundational because through their message we encounter Jesus Christ as Lord and Saviour.

In recognising the inspiration of Scripture, the Church accepted the authority of the Bible as the ultimate deciding factor on issues of true Christian belief and discipleship. It did not bestow authority but recognised it and placed itself in submission to 'God's word written'.

History provides many examples of the Church searching the Scriptures for guidance when dealing with crises and heresies. It also records numerous occasions when the Christian community has been recalled to faith and discipleship by the Spirit through the biblical message. The content of Scripture has provided a court of appeal and a bar of judgement before which believers have stood, and continue to stand, individually and as the people of God. For countless people, the Bible has proved its value as the reliable guidebook of both Christian faith and practice.

■ **John 10:35b; 21:24; Acts 28:25b; 2 Timothy 3:16-17; 2 Peter 1:3-4**

Scripture and other authorities

Scripture, Spirit and Church

The Bible, then, is the major authority for the Christian. However, the Bible itself teaches that there are three pillars which provide a secure foundation for Christian faith and practice. These three are: the teaching of Scripture, the direct illumination of the Holy Spirit and the consensus of the Christian community. The Bible is not safely used without reference to the general understanding of the Christian community throughout history, any more than it is understood without the help of the Spirit.

Jesus himself bore witness to the threefold foundation of our faith and in so doing, he instituted a guide and safeguard for his followers. Each of these three foundational sources requires the authentication of the other two to ensure that gospel truth is maintained.

In the New Testament, we possess a precious portrayal of Jesus and a witness to his transforming impact upon the lives of his first followers. Their words remain the measuring rod for Christian experience, orthodox belief and ethical conduct, but to read them correctly we need the guidance of the Holy Spirit. He breathes through the word and brings its truth to light, interpreting God's eternal message to our contemporary situation. We also need the confirmation of the Christian community. Throughout the centuries, the gospel of Jesus has been preached by his followers and their witness provides a key to understanding the Bible.

So the Christian has three authorities for understanding God's word and applying it: Scripture, Spirit and Church. Each authority confirms and sanctions the other two.

■ **John 15:26-27; Acts 15:22-29; 1 Thessalonians 5:12-22; 1 Timothy 4:6**

The primary authority

Within these three, however, the Bible remains the primary authority. Certainly the Spirit must breathe through the word and bring its truth to light, as it must resonate with the authentic witness of the historic Church. History teaches that both the claimed illumination of the Spirit and the traditions of the Church, when unchallenged, can be open to abuse. Historically, the teaching of the Church has sometimes been distorted by corrupt institutional structures. At times the guidance of the Spirit has been misapprehended, counterfeited or falsely claimed as a new private illumination.

Scripture, however, contains the experience of the Church as well as that of individual prophets and apostles. There is an inner coherence in the message, which affirms its authenticity. By comparing Scripture with Scripture an agreement may be discerned so that the will of God is clarified. Interpretation can never be concluded, for as we search the Scriptures, we enter into dialogue with them and experience the transforming power of the message, which speaks with encouragement and correction to our own situation. Scripture is its own interpreter.

Scripture as a whole provides the final court of appeal for the Christian. Its authority supercedes all other claims, and its teaching authenticates all other spiritual truth. It is the underlying foundation upon which Christian consensus must rest, and it is the measure by which claimed illumination by the Spirit must be tested. To be accounted Christian, all other sources must conform to its essential, central teaching. In this sense, the Scriptures alone, '*they only* constitute the divine rule of Christian faith and practice.'

■ **Luke 24:25-27; John 5:39-40; 12:47-50; Acts 2:22-36**

Pluralism

Many of us live in pluralistic societies, where other sacred writings, an amalgamation of religious ideas and humanist philosophies compete for the hearts and minds of our communities. In this setting, we continue to maintain that for the Christian the Bible is the only authority to define belief and direct conduct.

The sacred writings of other religions may possess insights helpful to spiritual questing, but the Bible contains the record of God's mission in Christ to save humanity, and the nature and scope of the salvation made available. It stands alone.

Human philosophies and popular schools of thought are to be judged in the light of the timeless truths expressed in Scripture. Therefore the saving truth in the Bible is not to be reduced or revised to conform to popular attitudes or current ideologies that deny or undermine the faith.

Scripture remains the only divine rule of Christian faith and practice because it presents and preserves God's unique and unrepeatable revelation of himself in Jesus Christ, who at one particular moment in history, came as his living Word. Because we accept the lordship of Jesus to whom the Bible bears witness, we accept the Scripture as an enduring authority with continuing relevance. To accept Jesus is to recognise the authority of the written word within which he is encountered. Jesus himself is Lord of the Scripture, and the Bible is invaluable essentially because it introduces us to him.

■ **Luke 4:16-21; 1 Corinthians 1:18-2:13**

A word for all time

In all matters relating to faith in Christ and the life lived by faith, in this world and the next, the Bible is utterly trustworthy and reliable. All that is necessary to knowledge of saving truth is found within its pages. It spells hope for the future for all those who need to hear the good news of Jesus Christ. It was called into being by the living Word of God inspiring the minds of men and women, and from its pages God's living Word continues to address us with authority and power.

A summary

> *We believe that the Scriptures of the Old and New Testaments were given by inspiration of God and that they are the only divine rule of Christian faith and practice.*

Appendix 1

Determining the Canon

The Bible is the result of a long process of the collection and compilation of many ancient documents which testify to the living God. During the first five centuries an accepted list, or canon, of authoritative writings was established under the guidance of the Holy Spirit.

The Canon of the Old Testament was agreed in various stages, culminating in 91 AD, with the Council of Jamnia. The gathering of Jewish elders acknowledged 39 books in the Hebrew Scriptures, made up of books of the Law, the Prophets and the Writings.

Certain writings known as *the Apocrypha* are also found in some translations of the Bible. These books were part of the Septuagint, the Greek translation of the Old Testament, but were not accepted into the Jewish Canon at Jamnia. The Apocrypha is accepted by most Protestant Churches 'for edification' but should not be used alone to substantiate Christian beliefs.

The first mention of all 27 books as comprising the *Canon of the New Testament* was in 367 AD. This was ratified by the Council of Carthage in 397 AD. The New Testament consists of the Gospels, the Acts of the Apostles, the Letters and the Revelation. The letters of Paul and others are the earliest written testimony to Jesus Christ, and the Gospels were written soon afterwards. (Note: the present division of our Bible into chapters and verses was adopted later, by the 16th century.)

During and following the apostolic era, other writings made their appearance and appeal. Many contain helpful teaching. These books, however, do not enjoy the authority of Scripture. Their authors themselves often recognised the unique value of the biblical books and appealed to Scripture to validate their own derived teaching. Spurious writings and false gospels were rejected because they failed to meet the threefold criteria of the Canon.

An understanding of the formation of the Canon shows how God has revealed himself through the process of history, inspiring the biblical writers with a true vision of his person and purpose. The basis of the Bible's authority lies in the witness of the Spirit to men and women of God throughout the ages. This gives the Bible an internal consistency, which reveals the truth of Jesus Christ.

Appendix 2

Infallibility and inerrancy

It is not easy to find an expression that does justice both to the divine inspiration of Scripture and also to the human terms of its authorship. Some Christians seek to express their convictions about the Bible by describing it as infallible; some speak of the inerrancy of Scripture.

Others do not find such terms helpful unless the terms are interpreted in a way which satisfactorily allows for the writers' own activity. For example, the term 'infallible' might be accepted as denoting the quality of not deceiving or misleading and thereby simply meaning that the Scriptures are wholly trustworthy and reliable. The term 'inerrant' may be accepted as meaning wholly true, and referring to the conviction that the teaching of Scripture is the utterance of a God whose word must be trusted implicitly.

The Salvation Army's statement of faith does not include any reference to the infallibility or inerrancy of Scripture. What we do affirm is that we can rely upon the Scriptures of the Old and New Testaments for instruction and guidance in matters of divine truth and the Christian life, because in Scripture we meet the inspired Word of God himself, Jesus Christ. The Holy Spirit who inspired the writers also illumines those who read its pages and leads them to faith.

CHAPTER TWO

The God who is never alone

The doctrine of the Trinity

Related Doctrines

We believe that there is only one God, who is infinitely perfect, the Creator, Preserver, and Governor of all things, and who is the only proper object of religious worship.

We believe that there are three persons in the Godhead – the Father, the Son and the Holy Ghost, undivided in essence and co-equal in power and glory.

We believe in one God who is at the same time three.

Belief in one God is known as monotheism. Christians worship this one God as Father, Son and Holy Spirit. This is the doctrine of the Trinity, which is essential to an understanding of God as revealed in the Bible, and is basic to the Christian faith.

Christian monotheism

Monotheism is the doctrine that there is only one God. This belief is not peculiar to Christianity. It is also the belief held by a large section of the world's population, including Jews, Muslims and Sikhs.

However, Christian monotheism has its own particular meaning and content. It is important to know both what it means and what it does not mean.

Christian monotheism means that the one God, eternal, supreme and personal, is revealed and known as Father, Son and Holy Spirit, an eternal tri-unity. God has always been, is and always will be Father, Son and Holy Spirit.

Christian monotheism does not mean that God resides in passive isolation. He is a God related to his creation, he is not a static being, unrelated and unmoved.

The great initiator, preserver and governor of all things interacts with his creation. The way in which God makes himself known and meets with his people is central to the Bible story.

■ **Exodus 3:1-6, 13-14; 34:6-7; Deuteronomy 6:4-5; 2 Kings 13:23; Jonah 3:10; Mark 12:29-31**

A God in fellowship

God is never alone. Within himself he enjoys perfect and full fellowship. Although he is always three, he is not three individuals who could be in competition or opposition. He is three persons, always united in being, attitude and action, a threefold God of love.

These three persons commune with one another. God relates within himself. God is himself a communion. He is always Father, Son and Holy Spirit, each one always in fellowship with the others.

Father, Son and Holy Spirit represent a dynamic circulation of life among equal persons without any authority or superiority of one over another. Any attempt to develop a false hierarchy of power and glory within the Trinity is to weaken the integrity of the Godhead and to undermine the complete unity of the persons.

The three-in-one definition attempts to describe a God who as Father creates, governs and sustains; as Son redeems, befriends and disciples; and as Holy Spirit sanctifies, counsels and empowers. In persons and work he is three: in personality and love he is one.

The three persons of the Trinity are continually revealing one another to us. The New Testament tells us that the Spirit bears witness to Jesus, Jesus Christ reveals the Father and testifies to the Spirit, the Father testifies to the Son.

God created humanity because love expressed in community is the very essence of his nature, not because of any incompleteness within himself. As human beings, we are created in the image of God with a nature to relate to one another. We reach our fulfilment only in community with him and with one another. Without him and without each other, we lack wholeness and the possibility of maturity through developing relationships.

God, then, is always in fellowship within himself and with us. The Bible witnesses to this truth, which is the foundation of the Christian doctrine of salvation and of Christian experience itself. An understanding of the Trinity helps us identify, and so avoid, many heresies. (*See appendix 3.*)

When we speak of the triune God as one, it is in the sense of his wholeness and togetherness, and when we speak of God as three, it is in the sense of his threefold nature.

■ **Matthew 11:25-27; 28:19; John 14:8-26; 15:26; 1 Corinthians 12:4-6; 2 Corinthians 13:14; Jude 20-21**

A God who makes himself known

God discloses his person and purposes as Father, Son and Holy Spirit in the unfolding revelation of Scripture and in his saving encounters with us.

Though God reveals himself in many ways, in the Bible he discloses himself through relationships and critical events. He reveals himself in his relationships with Israel. He makes himself known through critical events, such as the Exodus, the rise and fall of the Hebrew kingdoms, the Exile and return, recorded in the Old Testament. In the New Testament, he makes himself known uniquely and supremely in the advent, life, crucifixion and resurrection of Jesus.

This self-disclosure agrees with human experience in which person is disclosed to person as relationships are entered and honoured and critical events shared. In the same way, God, who is personal and respects human personality, discloses his nature and his love for us.

We speak of God's self-disclosure because it is the nature of God to make himself known. God is love, and it is the characteristic of love to seek to be known to the loved one.

■ **Genesis 18:1-3; Psalm 19:1-6; Psalm 126; Psalm 136; Hosea 11:1-4; Luke 1:67-75; John 3:16; Romans 1:18-23; 1Corinthians 15:3-8; Galatians 3:25-4:6; Philippians 2:5-11**

A God involved with us

We believe that God is not distant from us but is involved with us. This is seen in the Incarnation, the coming of God as a human being, Jesus of Nazareth.

In the atonement for sin brought about by our Lord Jesus Christ in obedience to the Father, we see God crossing barriers to save the lost. This atonement makes possible the restoration of our relationship with God. (*See chapter 7.*)

God's involvement and initiative are further expressed in the gracious work of the Holy Spirit in regeneration and sanctification, which transforms our lives. (*See chapters 8 and 9.*) God is not indifferent. He is involved in human experience and is concerned to nurture human life.

■ **Exodus 34:1-10; Nehemiah 9:9-17; Psalm 103:1-14; Jonah 4:1-11; Luke 1:30-33, 46-55; Romans 5:6-11; 2 Corinthians 5:19; Titus 3: 4-7**

The character of God

When we meet God we meet him in his completeness. The triune God is of one undivided essence or being. The God we meet in Scripture and in our human experience makes himself known to us as the loving God who is holy, jealous, faithful, merciful and true.

God is *holy*. As the one who is altogether different, the uncreated source of all being, he evokes our awe. To acknowledge the holiness of God is to become aware of his utter goodness and purity.

■ **Leviticus 19:2; 1 Samuel 2:2; Isaiah 6:3; Revelation 4:8; 15:4**

God is *jealous*. His love entails a desire that we love him in return with single-hearted devotion. God cares so much for his people that he can never be indifferent to their unfaithfulness.

■ **Exodus 20:2-6; 34:14; Deuteronomy 4:24; Luke 13:34-35; 2 Corinthians 11:1-3**

God is *faithful*. Throughout Scripture he is shown to be unswerving in his covenantal love and commitment, however much and however often we may fail him.

■ **Deuteronomy 32:4; Psalm 89:1-37; 1 Corinthians 1:9; 10:13; 1 Thessalonians 5:23-24; Hebrews 10:23**

God is *merciful*. He shows mercy to all and delights in pardoning those who turn to him, trusting in his love and forbearance.

■ **Psalm 51:1-17; Luke 15:11-24; Ephesians 2:1-10; 1 Peter 1:3-5**

God is *true*. He is always consistent with his character of love and righteousness. He is the source, ground and author of ultimate truth and justice.

■ **Psalm 19:7-11; John 7:28-29; 1 John 5:20; Revelation 3:7; 19:11**

The glory of God

When we meet this God, we meet one who transcends our human limitations, both our finite human nature and the sinfulness that inclines us to idolatry. We meet a God who is exalted above powers and philosophies, over space and time, and yet whose awesome presence can be apprehended by those who love him. The glory of God is seen most clearly in Jesus Christ and is experienced in the life and worship of the redeemed community, the Church.

■ **Exodus 24:15-18; Ezekiel 1:26-28; John 1:14; 17:1-5; 2 Corinthians 4:3-6**

The human response: worship

It is this God whom alone we worship. In worship we recognise and give worth to what is central in our lives. We express where our full allegiance lies. As Christians we declare our complete allegiance to the triune God. This declaration is the backbone of our faith and unalterably identifies the God who is worshipped.

Christian worship is our wholehearted response to the God who is eternally in community, living and acting, relating to his creation, known by his works and revealed by his saving activity: Father, Son and Holy Spirit.

Worship begins when God makes himself known to us through his presence and his word, and by so doing makes possible the community of faith. It is completed when we express our gratitude, respond in faith, enter into spiritual fellowship and live the life of God in mission in the world.

The Lord Jesus confirmed the centrality of worship by his own practice and teaching. This was seen in his attendance at synagogue and in his personal prayer life; in his assertion that the Father seeks true worshippers; and in the way he linked worship with obedience to God's will. The apostle Paul also taught that the principle of worship was to be expressed in the consecration of our entire lives to God.

■ **1 Chronicles 29:10-13; Psalm 96:1-13; Matthew 5:23-24; Luke 4:16-21, 42; John 4:21-24; Romans 12:1-2**

In worship we respond to who God is.

◆ The glory of God evokes our adoration.

◆ The holiness of God evokes our awe.

◆ The jealousy of God evokes our exclusive devotion.

◆ The love of God evokes our sense of worth.

In worship we respond to what God does.

◆ The saving action of God evokes our response in gratitude.

◆ The seeking God evokes our response in prayer.

◆ The sanctifying God evokes our response in consecration.

◆ The merciful God evokes our response in penitence.

◆ The community-making God evokes our response in fellowship.

◆ The loving God evokes our response in compassionate evangelism and service.

Worship is life-changing. It helps worshippers move from fear to love, guilt to forgiveness, weakness to power, irresponsibility to stewardship, insecurity to trust, spiritual hunger to fullness of joy, sorrow to comfort, confusion to direction.

The danger of idolatry

Idolatry is worship offered or allegiance shown to false deities, demonic powers or material objects or values.

In the Bible, idolatry is forbidden by the second commandment and is continually condemned in both the Old Testament and the New. It was the target both of Old Testament prophets, and of Christian preachers when they moved into the pagan world of the Roman Empire.

Today idolatry remains a persistent and pernicious enemy of true religion. It sometimes takes the form of traditional ways of worshipping objects and images and in the fear which they evoke. It is also seen in more subtle ways, in the worship of the state, of wealth, of status, race, other individuals, or other concepts.

It is an ever-present danger to the Christian who must never divert to religious movements or leaders the worship and adoration that is due to God alone.

To guard against idolatry, we must focus on Jesus. By doing this we will be reminded of the glory of the Father who is revealed in the Son. The Holy Spirit will help us to resist all temptation to give to any other person or power that ultimate devotion which is due to God alone.

■ **Exodus 20:4-6; Hosea 14:8-9; 1 Corinthians 10:14; Colossians 3:5; 1 John 5:21**

A God to make known

We believe that as it is in the nature of God to reveal himself, it is the calling of Christians to make him known. God is the source of all love; he is the foundation upon which all longings for true human community are built. To be found by him is to know oneself loved by the one, true, merciful and faithful God. To find him is to be aware of his glory and moved to worship and praise. It is this God who calls us to share in his mission and tell his story.

A summary

We believe that there is only one God, whom alone we worship, eternally existing in three co-equal persons, of one essence, Father, Son and Holy Spirit.

Appendix 3

Wrong paths – trinitarian heresies

The Christian faith is simple, but Christian theology arising from it is not. It is not surprising that misunderstandings have arisen during the nearly two-thousand-year history of the Church. The historic creeds are the result of efforts to correct distortions of the apostolic faith, which is the faith proclaimed by the apostles to which the New Testament bears witness. It was handed on in the Early Church and eventually shaped the universally accepted creeds. (*See appendix 11.*)

Historically, impulses to correct trinitarian excesses at one extreme have sometimes resulted in heretical views at the other. Most trinitarian heresies can be classified under one of the following three types:

Modalism – the belief that the one God projects himself in three ways or modes. This is caused by the impulse to avoid the idea of three gods but results in the loss of the relationship between three distinct persons.

Tritheism – the belief that the three persons have different characteristics, desires and objectives. This arises from the impulse to protect the integrity and identity of the three persons but results in the loss of the oneness of God's attitude and action.

Subordinationism – the belief that the Father is eternally superior to the Son and the Spirit. Causes of this may include a projection of a society's hierarchical structure, or a desire to equate the Father with other monotheistic deities.

Other wrong paths include:

Polytheism – belief in many gods. This is denied by the unmistakable Scriptural command to have no other gods.

Deism – the belief that God is a remote First Cause who brought the universe into being but left it to run as a machine. This is denied by the scriptural doctrine of God's involvement with his creation.

Pantheism – the belief that God and creation are one without distinction. Pantheistic teachings are prevalent in many New Age movements, whose subtlety and diversity can cause confusion.

New Age – an umbrella name for many forms of neo-paganism that combine the mysticism and spiritism of some eastern religions and ancient mythologies, with belief in the unlimited potential of human beings to determine their own destiny. Its techniques are designed to increase self-awareness, leading to divinity. New Age recognises no distinction in kind between God and humanity: the spiritual facility in all human beings, fully exploited, is thought to be sufficient to bring in a new age of peace and love. This approach is characteristic of tendencies to dilute Christian truth by combining it with other philosophies and religions.

CHAPTER THREE

Creator of Heaven and earth

The doctrine of God the Father

Related Doctrines

We believe that there is only one God, who is infinitely perfect, the Creator, Preserver and Governor of all things, and who is the only proper object of religious worship.

We believe that there are three Persons in the Godhead – the Father, the Son and the Holy Ghost, undivided in essence and co-equal in power and glory.

We believe that God is the creator of the world and sustains it by his gracious purpose. The world and all that is in it was created fundamentally good because it was brought into being by a holy, wise, powerful and loving God.

God the Father

The picture of God as a father can be found in the Old Testament. But it is in the New Testament that God's fatherhood is given prominence through the teaching of Jesus.

He taught that God is Father and his own relationship with God is described in the intimate designation, 'Abba, Father'. God the Father is the one with whom Jesus enjoyed unimpaired fellowship and to whom he offered complete loving obedience. He is the Father in whom Jesus trusted when tempted in Gethsemane, and to whom he could surrender his spirit when dying on the Cross. The Son was raised from death through the glory of the Father. Through Jesus Christ, he is our Father, too.

Like Jesus, therefore, we now have a relationship with God similar to that of a child with his father. The writings of Paul and others, endorse the intimate words of the Lord Jesus. As Paul says: '. . . you received the Spirit of sonship. And by him we cry, *"Abba, Father"*'(Romans 8:15).

Some have encountered problems with this doctrine. For example, some focus unduly on the maleness of the Father. The scriptural description of God as father does not mean that God is a male, but rather that he acts towards us as a loving father would. The Bible also describes God as loving us with the tenderness and loving care associated with motherhood.

Another difficulty is that human fatherhood is too often a travesty of true paternity. Even when faithful and loving, it is imperfect. There is evidence that the Lord Jesus was aware of this difficulty but regarded it as surmountable, for he said that though human fathers were faulty they still gave good gifts to their children, and pointed to a perfect divine fatherhood that would give to those who asked in faith.

Jesus' own life and character defines his meaning, for he tells us that to have seen him is to have seen the Father. To worship God through Jesus is to know the fatherly relationship of compassion and care for which human beings long. The almighty creator, the eternal God revealed in the Old Testament, is the 'Abba, Father' to whom we come through Jesus Christ.

God is our Father because he is the Father of Jesus Christ, who is our Lord. Though the whole creation, including all humanity, issues from God, this fatherly relationship is the special inheritance of Christian believers.

■ **Deuteronomy 32:6; Isaiah 63:16; Malachi 2:10; Matthew 6:7-33; Mark 14:36; Luke 11:5-13; 23:46; Romans 6:4; 8: 14-17; Galatians 3:26-4:7**

Creator of Heaven and earth

Creation out of nothing

We believe that God created the world. 'In the beginning, God created the heavens and the earth' (Genesis 1:1). In this text, 'the beginning' does not refer to God, for he is eternal, without beginning or end. The reference is to the universe which is given birth by his will and purpose. In proclaiming that God made all things, we assert that the universe had a beginning: matter has not always existed. God brought it into being by his sovereign will expressed in his word. 'God said, "Let there be . . ." . . . . And it was so.' Creation was out of nothing by the word of God.

The universe and all it contains possesses dignity and meaning because it is not the result of chance or accident. It is the expression of divine intent and authority, which gives delight to its creator. The creation account in the first chapter of the Bible portrays a progression from dark chaos to luminous harmony and an ordered procession of events which culminated in the creation of human beings, male and female, made in the image of God.

God's creative power is not confined to the visible and material. All spiritual powers, even those presently opposed to God, owe their existence to him. The biblical revelation denies all suggestion that matter is inherently evil and that the physical is opposed to the spiritual. All is the creation of the one God, and the Church has rejected teaching which suggested otherwise. Such dualistic philosophies have sometimes corrupted monotheistic religions by teaching that equal opposing forces of good and evil, God and Satan, are locked in unending conflict. Christian teaching recognises the power of evil, but claims that ultimately God is sovereign and his creation good. 'God saw all that he had made, and it was very good' (Genesis 1:31).

The Christian distinguishes between God and his creation. The world is not an emanation from the divine Being. God is present in all, but all is not God. We believe in the God who is both involved with his creation and distinct from it.

■ **Genesis 1; Psalm 33:6; Psalm 93; Isaiah 45:12; John 1:1-3; Colossians 1:15-17; Hebrews 11:3**

The problem of evil

We do not possess a logical explanation of the existence of evil in a universe created by a God of love. Both human wickedness and natural disaster pose enormous problems for Christians. There is a temptation to ascribe all such evil to the malevolence of Satan, but while referring to Satan and his angels may shed some light, it does not fully illuminate the problem. Scripture offers no explanation of the problem of irrational evil but teaches that God is in control. Ultimately, even opposing powers conform to his plans although against their will.

Evil that arises from the wickedness of human beings can be seen as a risk of our creation as free, personal beings, made in the image of God. We were made to respond freely to the love of God, a freedom that must include the freedom to refuse. God's plan to save us from the frightening consequences of rejecting him led to the Cross. (*See chapter 7.*)

■ Genesis 3; 45:5-8; Job 1; 12:23; Isaiah 45:1-7; Romans 1:18-32; Ephesians 1:9-10; Colossians 1:19-20

Preserver and governor

God has not ceased his creative activity. Creation is changing and the universe is developing. God is creatively bringing his world to the fullness he intends for it. The New Testament witnesses that through means both gradual and traumatic we are being prepared for a new Heaven and a new earth.

In this sense God is both preserver and governor of all he has made. Preservation of the created order does not mean maintenance of the status quo but rather preservation of his ongoing purpose and unfolding plan for creation. Just as all spiritual powers, even those opposed to God, owe their existence to him, so also God is ultimately governor of all rulers and authorities, even though for the present they may appear to be operating outside of the boundaries of his control.

The purposes of God are the final reference point for all human endeavour. In our planning, our designs for the future, we are all accountable to God. This is a source of confidence and hope. We can be secure in God's loving care, even in the presence of so much that seeks to harm us. In the face of unexplainable evil or suffering, we know that we are firmly in the hands of a loving creator God.

■ Job 34:14-15; Psalm 65:9-13, 104:24-30; Isaiah 65:17-25; John 19:11; Romans 8:18-25; Colossians 1:17; Revelation 21:1-4

Caring for God's world

God's authority over the created order does not mean rigid and overbearing control but rather a caring, dynamic, interactive relationship with his creation. He works in co-operation with his creation to fulfil his purposes for it. He is in control, but invites us to share responsibility for his world.

The relationship of God to his creation is one of loving care and concern. Humanity's stewardship of the earth is a reflection of that care, as human beings are made in the image of God. Our creator has given us responsibility to care for his creation. We have the freedom to take the raw materials of the universe and work them into good for present and future generations. That freedom should not be abused. Our challenge is to treat the earth well in the light of increasing population and diminishing resources.

The world was made to praise God and reveal his glory: our stewardship of it furthers that end.

■ **Genesis 1:29-31; Psalm 8; 19:1-6**

Perfect in holiness

A feeling of awe in the presence of God is common to religious experience. We reach out to that which is different from ourselves, to complete purity and goodness, not simply to greater power. What we are recognising is the holiness of God. Our sense of awe is often accompanied by an awareness of guilt and unworthiness in the presence of divine holiness.

From beginning to end, the Bible testifies to the holiness of God. From an early understanding of God's otherness that is sometimes expressed in alarming terms, the Bible moves to a profound perception of the awe-inspiring nature of his goodness and righteousness. It is this holiness, this separateness, which differentiates God from us. It is this divine quality which draws us to him in worship.

■ **Psalm 111:9; Isaiah 5:16; 6:1-7; 57:15; Matthew 6:9; Revelation 4:1-11**

Perfect in wisdom

While the holiness of God reminds us of his otherness, that is, his transcendence over his creation, the wisdom of God points to his engagement with us. By exercise of his wisdom, God directs all that happens towards the fulfilment of his purposes. God is actively involved in and with all that he has made, and his wisdom is constantly at work to bring all people to himself.

Old Testament writers saw God's wisdom at work in all his tireless activity. Wisdom was employed at creation and revealed in God's works and in the ordering of the world. In his wisdom, God gave the Law to enable his people to live in right relationship with him. The teaching of Jesus fully expresses God's wisdom and the person of Christ fully embodies it.

God knows all things and is alongside us as the future unfolds. His knowledge is not dispassionate; he not only knows us, but he is also involved with us.

His wise and loving understanding of us is constantly directed towards our good.

■ **Proverbs 8:22-36; Jeremiah 10:12; Romans 11:33-36; 1 Corinthians 1:18-31; Colossians 2:3**

Perfect in power

Throughout Scripture, God's power is seen at work for our good. It is revealed in creation, in the great events of Hebrew history and is described vividly by the prophets. In the creeds, God is described as 'the Father Almighty'. By his power, God leads the world towards his own goals. While allowing his creation a measure of freedom, God remains ultimately sovereign and works through all events towards the fulfilment of his purposes.

In the New Testament, Christ is called the power of God. The Cross reveals the deepest dimensions of God's power in the apparent weakness which disarms the powers of darkness and the agencies of evil, so accomplishing our salvation. Here God demonstrates the power of suffering love.

■ **Isaiah 40:18-31; Romans 1:16; 1 Corinthians 1:24; 2 Corinthians 12:7-10; Ephesians 6:10-11**

Perfect in love

We believe in God whose love cannot be defined in terms of passing emotion, indulgence or cheap and vague benevolence.

In the Old Testament the love of God is first and foremost his steadfast burning faithfulness to his people, Israel, his covenant love. Though constantly betrayed, God continued in loving faithfulness to lead his people towards holiness. In the New Testament, the faithfulness of God is shown in the giving of his Son Jesus Christ whose willing obedience revealed the extent of the love of God. In that gift, which displays the intimate relationship and complete harmony of God the Father with God the Son, we see God's perfect love. That love determines the nature of divine holiness, wisdom and power.

It is God's steadfast love that informs and directs his purposes and empowers his will. His love reaches out to all, whether responsive or impenitent: a covenant love, confirmed by promise and perseverance. It is an unconditional love.

■ **Isaiah 49:15-16; 54:4-10; Jeremiah 31:3-5; Hosea 3:1; John 17:23; Romans 5:8; 1 John 4:16**

Love and power

Two illuminating aspects of true love are its self-communication and its self-denial.

Those who love must in the very nature of things express love creatively. They must convey their love by both revealing and perpetuating themselves. For there is no true love where there is no confidence of self-worth, with a consequent desire to express and replicate that worth. At the same time, those who love also deny themselves, giving worth and priority to the beloved.

If we recognise that God is love, then we acknowledge that he must express himself both in the affirmation and the denial of himself. His will can only be expressed by a simultaneous self-assertion and self-denial. Our own experiences of life enable us to see how God's love defines his power. Simply to look for an unrestrained show of force fails to recognise the creative power of love. God's power, put at risk by the constraints of his love, demonstrates its creativity in the gift of his Son.

Jesus' death on the Cross is the greatest demonstration of divine love, both in terms of utter self-denial and entire self-affirmation. God's suffering love, which has transformed countless lives, is the best argument for the validity of this understanding of his power.

■ **Psalm 22:1-3, 23-25; Isaiah 52:13-53:12; Mark 15:33-34; 1 Peter 2:20-24**

Love, power and suffering

Any affirmation of God's power and his love inevitably invites the question, 'Why does he allow suffering?' Much suffering appears cruel and pointless and no attempts at rational explanation are satisfactory. Sometimes the only real comfort comes from the assurance of the presence of a loving God who in Jesus fully entered into our present suffering. He is present in the midst of such suffering so that no-one need suffer alone.

We may be helped by the insight that suffering is part of life in a fallen world. It is the cost of life, as growing and insight cost pain. To gain maturity, wisdom and knowledge involves a measure of suffering. Pain and suffering are part of love and the cost of love is vulnerability. Christians are called to embody this vulnerable presence by standing with, and sharing the pain of, those who suffer.

On the Cross, God in Christ shared our suffering and, though no longer suffering to atone, he still shares human anguish. Such love must suffer. This understanding does not remove the bitterness of experience but addresses the apparent meaninglessness which makes suffering more acute. While no easy answers are given to the questions suffering raises, the Cross provides the most penetrating insight into the true nature of experience. It is a pointer to a plan presently hidden from understanding and a clue to the value of suffering in human lives.

■ **Job 42:1-6; Psalm 116:1-5; 130; Luke 24:25-27; Romans 5:3-5; 8:17-19, 31-39; 2 Corinthians 1:3-7**

A love to be shared

We best understand the love of God in relation to his revelation in Jesus Christ. This helps us to see that God's holiness, wisdom and power are defined by his eternal love. For in God holiness is an expression of pure love, wisdom is an expression of love at work, power is an expression of costly love. This love, embodied in Jesus Christ, is the love God invites us to share with the world.

A summary

We believe in God the Father, creator of Heaven and earth, preserver and governor of all, perfect in holiness, wisdom, power and love.

CHAPTER FOUR

God's eternal Son

The doctrine of Jesus Christ

Related Doctrines

We believe that there are three persons in the Godhead – the Father, the Son and the Holy Ghost, undivided in essence and co-equal in power and glory.

We believe that in the person of Jesus Christ the Divine and human natures are united, so that He is truly and properly God and truly and properly man.

We believe that the Lord Jesus Christ has by His suffering and death made an atonement for the whole world so that whosoever will may be saved.

Faith in Jesus Christ as Lord and Saviour is central to Christian experience and witness. We believe in Jesus Christ – the second person in the Trinity – who reigns in full communion with God the Father and with the Holy Spirit. God sent Jesus to rescue our fallen world. We recognise God's perfect will and purpose in his birth, life, death and resurrection, his ascension and his second coming. In his whole life history we hear God's living word and we see God's glory.

■ **John 17: 1-5; Romans 10: 9-13; 1 Timothy 3:16**

Jesus the man

Our doctrine speaks of Jesus as 'truly and properly God and truly and properly man'. As we explore this mystery, we look first at Jesus of Nazareth, whose true humanity was as our own, and whose story is recorded for us in the Gospels. Jesus was a real human being, whose historical existence can be upheld and whose true humanity is clearly shown.

A historical figure

Jesus lived two thousand years ago, and the Gospels as well as other sources tell us about him. He was a Jew living in Palestine when it was a province of the Roman Empire. In the Gospel of Luke, the account of his birth is linked to events in the time of Caesar Augustus. His life and his death on the Cross are referred to in other ancient manuscripts. His whole life and ministry must be seen in the context of Jewish religious life and history. Though his universal message and ministry broke the boundaries of Judaism, he belonged to the Jewish/Roman world of the first century AD.

We believe that Jesus was a historical person. In him, God has revealed himself and acted in history for us. If Jesus did not live, he did not die for our salvation, nor was he raised by God. Without the Jesus of history, there is no Christ of faith.

A real human being

We believe that Jesus' true humanity is clearly revealed in the Bible. The Gospels describe how Jesus shared normal human faculties. He felt hunger and thirst and weariness; experienced delight, anger and grief, affection and compassion. He developed from childhood to adulthood. He learned facts by observation and could be surprised and horrified. He bled and died. In addition, the Gospels witness to the significance of his prayer life, the reality of his temptations, the importance he gave to Scripture and the role of community and religious tradition in his growth and development. He was fully human.

The New Testament reveals Jesus to be a man of true humanity. His love for God, compassion for all people, personal freedom and moral integrity reveal to us the kind of life that God intended for all human beings. He is the true man.

A unique human being

In the fully human life of Jesus we are confronted with the biblical witness to his perfection. He is the true image of God for, alone among all human beings, Jesus lived without sin. This must be understood in the context of the work of God in him and of his unique relationship with God the Father. The very closeness of that relationship exposed him more intensely to all the realities of temptation, to real conflict with the powers of darkness, to suffering, isolation and death. In that loving relationship he was able to resist temptation and remain sinless, even to the point of death on the Cross.

■ **Matthew 4:1-11; Mark 1:41; 11:12; 14:32-42; Luke 2:52; 4:1-21; John 4:6; 11:35; 14:1-11; 17:1-5; Hebrews 2:10-18; 5:1-10**

Jesus, God's Son

The Incarnation

Jesus Christ was not only true man, but 'truly and properly God'. 'He was with God in the beginning. Through him all things were made . . .' (John 1:2-3). The character and being of God were fully present in the life of the man Jesus, for 'He who has seen me has seen the Father' (John 14: 9). The early Christians adopted the word 'Incarnation' to describe this truth. The word is not strictly a biblical term, but literally means 'embodiment' or 'in the flesh' (John 1:14). The doctrine of the Incarnation declares that our God became one of us, though without sin.

This truth is expressed in different ways by the New Testament writers. In the Gospel of John we read that 'the Word became flesh and lived for a while among us' (John 1:14). In Philippians, Paul expresses this truth when he describes Christ as 'being in very nature God', and yet 'taking the very nature of a servant'. (Philippians 2:6-7). In Hebrews, Jesus Christ is referred to as 'the radiance of God's glory and exact representation of his being' (Hebrews 1:3). A number of names and titles taken from the language of the Old Testament and from the first-century world are brought to the aid of those seeking to express in relevant language the inexpressible mystery of the fullness of God present in Jesus Christ. (*See appendix 5.*)

The doctrine of the Incarnation was formally developed in the Early Church as Christians pondered the record of the New Testament, experienced the presence of Christ in their worship and found it necessary to respond to doctrinal errors. At the Council of Chalcedon in 451, a statement was formulated which embraced the twin truths that Jesus Christ is one integrated person, with a divine and a human nature, 'without confusion, without change, without division, without separation . . . at once complete in Godhead and complete in manhood, truly God and truly man' (from the *Chalcedonian Definition*). In the person of Jesus we see humanity fully open to divine grace and we see God revealed to us.

■ **John 1:1-5, 14-18; 2 Corinthians 8:9; Philippians 2:5-11; Colossians 1:15-17; Hebrews 1:1-3**

The Virgin Birth

In the Gospels of Matthew and Luke we read about the conception of Jesus by the Holy Spirit. Like all human beings, Jesus was born of a woman, Mary, whose obedience to God opened the way for his outpouring of grace in the person of Jesus. But Jesus' person, life and character cannot be explained solely in terms of human heredity. God was at work in Jesus from the moment of conception. This conviction is bound up with his conception by the Holy Spirit and his birth to Mary, usually referred to as the doctrine of the Virgin Birth.

The doctrine of the Virgin Birth illuminates our understanding of the nature of the Lord Jesus Christ. It asserts his divinity as well as his advent in time as a man, made in the image of God. It reminds us that Jesus is both like us and unlike us.

■ **Matthew 1:18-25; Luke 1:26-38**

Jesus Christ our Lord

'Jesus is Lord' is the earliest credal statement found in the New Testament. It testifies to the deity of Jesus Christ, that he is one with the Father, sharing the Father's very being and fulfilling the Father's mission. The disciples recognised in their risen and ascended Lord the true image, presence and power of God. Through their experience, they realised that worship given to him was as given to God. The confession that Jesus is Lord is the mark of the true Christian believer, for 'everyone who calls upon the name of the Lord will be saved' (Romans 10:13).

■ **Joel 2:32; Matthew 14:22-33; Matthew 17:1-8; Luke 5:1-11; John 20:26-28; Philippians 2:10-11**

Salvation story

Christianity is a historical faith. The New Testament, especially the four Gospels, tells the story of Jesus. The major creeds also provide an outline of his life history. To tell the story is to preach the gospel, for the Christian faith is based upon what has actually happened in the life, death and resurrection of Jesus Christ. It is also the story of our salvation.

The public ministry of Jesus followed his baptism in the River Jordan. Filled with the Holy Spirit, Jesus set out to teach and to preach the good news of the Kingdom. He taught that the time had come for God's reign to be established: his very coming had brought the Kingdom near. All people, especially the poor and the outcasts, were invited to share in the celebrations. With great authority, he called disciples to follow him. He healed the sick and oppressed. He challenged and defeated the power of evil as a sign of the coming Kingdom. But Jesus' actions also challenged the religious authorities of his day, who sought to kill him. Jesus believed that his suffering and death were within the will and purposes of God. He did not yield to the temptation to avoid the bitterness of suffering and death.

■ **Matthew 4:23-25; Mark 1:14-3:6; 14:32-52; Luke 11:14-23; John 12:27-28**

Thus, *the death of Jesus* was no accident or tragic mistake. Jesus did not give up his life as a victim suffering for a cause. He died on the Cross fully trusting that through his death, and by his obedience to God, the purposes of God his Father would be fulfilled. His arrest and trial by the religious authorities, the death sentence imposed by the Roman government, the terrible crucifixion he endured, his death and burial in a borrowed grave – these were not the meaningless events they appeared to be at the time to his followers. Though they were

40

due to the actions of sinful people, it became evident that God was at work through Jesus in all that happened, and the offering of his life was God's gift to the world.

■ **Matthew 16:21-27; Mark 8:27-34; Luke 9:22; John 10:17-18, 11:49-52; Acts 2:22-23; Romans 5:15-19**

The death of Jesus was not the end of the story. The whole New Testament resounds with the proclamation that God raised Jesus from the dead. *The resurrection of our Lord Jesus Christ* in bodily form turned apparent failure into triumph and confirmed the power of self-giving love over evil and death. God's transforming presence is truly among us: Jesus is exalted as Lord and Christ.

The New Testament presents the resurrection as the fulfilment of prophecy. It is a moment in history to which the empty tomb gave witness. It is a fact of experience signified by the meeting of the risen Christ with his apostles and other believers. It is the Kingdom of God bursting through by the power of the Holy Spirit. It is also our assurance of life to come in all the fullness that God wills for us.

No satisfactory explanation of the birth of Christianity can be given without taking seriously the conviction born in the disciples that their Lord was risen from the dead. The existence of the Church, Christ's living body on earth, is evidence of his risen life.

■ **Matthew 28:5-6; Mark 16:1-7; Luke 24:1-9; John 20:16-18; 1 Corinthians 15:3-8**

The ascension of the Lord Jesus signified the end of his post-resurrection appearances recorded in the Gospels, and the return of the Son to the glory eternally shared with the Father and the Holy Spirit. It also prepared for the Church's understanding of Christ's continuing ministry as intercessor in Heaven.

The return of Christ is an integral part of the gospel as proclaimed in the New Testament. Jesus himself warned against speculation about dates and times, but we look forward expectantly to Christ's ultimate triumph; we pray for his return and prepare ourselves for the consummation of God's purposes through the return of his Son. (*See chapter 11.*)

■ Matthew 6:10; 26:64; Luke 24:50-52; Acts 1:6-11; 1 Corinthians 15:23-24; Colossians 3:4; 1 Thessalonians 4:13-18; 2 Thessalonians 2:1-4; Revelation 22:7, 20

Our salvation story

In the life, death and resurrection of Jesus we find the story which proclaims the reality of our redemption. His life is our salvation story.

Jesus' whole life centred on his relationship with God the Father. He lived in the joy of God's presence and trusted him so completely that his life was fully open to those around him. He loved God wholeheartedly and was completely obedient to his will, even to the point of suffering and death. It is this kind of self-forgetfulness that is the real measure of human wholeness. In the example of Jesus we see our pattern for living.

The loving obedience of Jesus was the means through which God reconciled the world to himself. We are part of that world. Salvation is to enter by faith into the story of Jesus, so that, associated with and transformed by his death and risen life, we may share the fruits of his self-giving.

Because Jesus is our Saviour, the story of Jesus is our salvation story.

■ Luke 24:13-35; John 3:16; 13:12-17; Acts 10:36-43; Romans 6:1-4; Hebrews 2:14-18; 1 Peter 2:21-25

A story to be told

The story belongs not only to us, it also belongs to the world. The story of the One is the story for everyone. Our mission is to tell the story with compelling passion.

A summary

We believe in Jesus Christ, God's eternal Son, conceived by the Holy Spirit, born of Mary. In him humanity and deity are united. He lived a perfect life, died an atoning death, was raised from the dead and lives at the right hand of the Father; he intercedes for his people and will return in power and glory.

Appendix 4

Wrong paths – Christological heresies

From the earliest times, distorted pictures of the person of Jesus Christ have emerged in the Church. These have usually arisen from a desire to explain and understand how Jesus could possibly be both true man and true God. Sometimes the pictures have over-emphasised the divinity of Christ, sometimes his humanity. The result has always been to undermine or destroy the person of Jesus that the Bible reveals. Many modern heresies have their origins in the ancient debates that were finally resolved at the Council of Chalcedon.

Arianism

In the fourth century, Arius taught that Jesus, though in some sense divine, was the first created being. He was not 'one with the Father' as the New Testament proclaims. (For example *see John 10:30; 14:9; 17:20-21.*) Later, other false pictures emerged. Apollinarius, also in the fourth century, taught that Jesus possessed the body of a man but the mind, or rational being, of God, that he was 'a miraculous mixture'. Nestorius, a century later, believed that Jesus had a human and a divine centre of being, in effect a divided person. Christian teaching eventually refuted Arius and the others by maintaining the total oneness of the Father and the Son and their eternal relationship.

Adoptionism

This belief, which also originated in the Early Church, maintained that Jesus was 'adopted' at some time in his human life as Son of God. It arose from a misinterpretation of Jesus' baptism experience. It is a denial of his pre-existence as declared in the New Testament.

Docetism

Docetic heresies affirm that the human body of Jesus was not real and only seemed to exist. Thus Jesus is understood as a divine being who inhabited the earth for a while in the guise of a man. This was a view held by many in the ancient world who could not believe that the divine could be associated with suffering. Docetism refuses to acknowledge the reality, and necessity for us, of Jesus' true humanity.

Ebionitism

The word derives from the Hebrew, meaning 'the poor', and was originally a name of honour in the early Palestinian churches. It also referred to an early Christian heresy, in some ways the converse of docetism. Some Jewish believers saw Jesus as a purely human figure, although recognizing that he was endowed with particular charismatic gifts which distinguished him from other humans.

A helpful reminder

All of this helps to remind us that there is no adequate theory of the Incarnation that can fully explain the mystery, 'God was in Christ reconciling the world to himself' (2 Corinthians 5:19, *RSV.*) The fullness of God was present in the man Jesus and thus the way was secured whereby all humanity could be united to God.

Appendix 5

The names and titles of Jesus

The New Testament speaks of Jesus Christ in a language of awe and wonder at the majesty and humility of God who has made himself known through him. Its writers searched for models from the Scripture and from their own world of meaning to describe Jesus, whom they had discovered to be central to their new understanding of God and of life. Some of these names and titles of Jesus Christ follow, though there are many more.

Lord

This title indicates that Jesus shares authority with God the Father, exercising sovereign power and deserving complete obedience. He is the Lord of all, acknowledged by those who put their trust in him.

■ Psalm 110:1; Acts 2:36; Romans 10:9

Christ

Christ is the Greek equivalent of 'Messiah', the Hebrew word meaning 'anointed one'. This term links the gospel to its Jewish beginnings for, to Jews, the Messiah was to inaugurate God's Kingdom on earth. Jesus transformed the concept while fulfilling the promise. After the resurrection, the followers of Jesus identified him as the Messiah, the Christ, to such a degree that what was first a title came to be regarded as a personal name of Jesus.

■ **Mark 1:1; 8:29; John 20:31**

Son of God

Jesus is the eternal Son of his Father God, in a loving relationship of obedience and trust, and in perfect tri-unity with the Father and the Holy Spirit.

■ **Romans 1:2-4**

Son of Man

Probably relating to Daniel's prophecy, this is Jesus' own self-description. It is united in his thinking with the concept of the Messiah and the suffering servant. Through the suffering, death and triumph of the Son of Man, the glory of God will be revealed for salvation.

■ **Daniel 7:13; Mark 10:33-34, 45; 14:61-62**

Saviour

God has given us Jesus to be the means of our salvation. The name 'Jesus' means 'one who saves'. This deliverance from the dominion of evil and death was achieved by him on behalf of all and is effective for the salvation of those who believe.

■ **Matthew 1:21**

Servant

Jesus is God's servant as the one who is perfectly obedient, and our servant as the one who willingly suffers with and for us. He described himself as the one who serves, and the Church saw him as the fulfilment of the prophecy of the suffering servant.

■ **Isaiah 52:13-53:12; Mark 10:45; Philippians 2:7; 1 Peter 2:21-25**

The Word

Jesus is the meaningful expression of God in creation and re-creation – the *Logos* which is translated Word. As the Word made flesh, he embodies the reality of God in human history.

■ **John 1:1-5, 14**

King

Jesus reigns with the Father over the Kingdom of God. His rule comprises a radical reversal of the values by which secular kingdoms operate.

■ **John 18:36-37**

Judge

Not only will Jesus return to judge the living and the dead, but also his costly love is a present judgement upon us and the supreme challenge to obedient faith.

■ **John 9:39; 2 Corinthians 5:10**

High Priest

Jesus is the one who sympathises with our weaknesses and who effectively intercedes for us with the Father. He is able to do this because of the atoning value of his outpoured life.

■ **Hebrews 4:14-16; 7:23-28**

Last Adam

Jesus is the one by whose obedience the consequences of the first Adam's disobedience are overthrown and the will of the Creator for humanity is both vindicated and fulfilled.

■ **1 Corinthians 15:45**

Head of the Body

Jesus Christ is the governor of the Church of which he is both the origin and completion.

■ **Ephesians 1:22-23; 4:15; Colossians 1:18**

CHAPTER FIVE

The Holy Spirit, Lord and giver of life

The doctrine of the Holy Spirit

Related Doctrines

We believe that there are three persons in the Godhead – the Father, the Son and the Holy Ghost, undivided in essence and co-equal in power and glory.

We believe that repentance towards God, faith in our Lord Jesus Christ, and regeneration by the Holy Spirit, are necessary to salvation.

To the Christian, the Holy Spirit is both a tender, intimate presence and a mystery beyond full understanding. He brings God near to us and directs our attention to Jesus. Although the Nicene Creed speaks of him as 'the Lord and Giver of life' the historic creeds are generally brief and reserved in their descriptions of his status and function. Nevertheless, a true understanding of the triune God requires a description of the third person of the Trinity and his work.

The Holy Spirit is the Spirit of Christ

The Holy Spirit glorifies the living Christ and presents him to us. Through his abiding presence and continuing ministry, we are made aware of the reality of the risen life of Jesus and are united in our relationship with him. He is the guarantor that Jesus is with us to the end of the age. Through the Spirit we stand alongside Jesus and cry, 'Abba, Father'. In this way the Spirit gives us our identity as brothers and sisters of Christ and confirms our relationship with the Father.

■ **John 14:16-18; 16:12-15; Romans 1:1-4; 8:15-17; Galatians 4:6; 1 John 4:2-3**

The Holy Spirit is Lord

Study of Scripture reveals that the Holy Spirit is the Spirit of God. He shares the divine attributes and activities and is given the title properly applied to God – the Lord. He is one with the Father and the Son, distinctive in person, yet one in essence.

For centuries Christians have searched for ways in which to describe the person of the Holy Spirit and the extension of his presence from the inner life of the Godhead to the experienced life of the Church. Most Christian churches affirm that the Holy Spirit proceeds from the Father and the Son, to emphasise the mutual relationship among the three persons in the Trinity. Eastern Orthodox churches have held that the Spirit proceeds only from the Father, to emphasise the distinctiveness of the Holy Spirit's person and role within the Godhead. All Christians uphold the co-equality of the three persons, however this may be expressed. Spirit, Son and Father are together as triune God.

■ **Psalm 139:1-12; John 14:26; 15:26; 20:22-23; Romans 8:9-11; 1 Corinthians 12:3; 2 Corinthians 3:17-18**

The Holy Spirit is free and powerful

In Scripture the presence of the Spirit is sometimes made known by such manifestations as wind, fire, or the form of a dove. The language of Scripture suggests an element of mystery and sovereign freedom. The presence of the Spirit is both tangible and intangible, invisible yet powerful.

Jesus taught that the Holy Spirit is not to be commanded or contained by individuals or structures. His illustration was that, as the wind has liberty to blow wherever it wills with its source and destination unknown, so the Holy Spirit achieves his will in unexpected and unpredictable ways. He is free of human manipulation or control.

Although the Holy Spirit is active in the Christian community, the Bible teaches that his activity is not confined to the life of the Church. No human group, whether defined by race, class or culture, is beyond his reach.

■ **Genesis 1:1-2; John 3:1-8; Acts 2:1-4; 10:34-48**

The Holy Spirit is the giver of life

In creation

The Creator acts by the movement of the Spirit. With energy like the wind, yet able to impose form and order, the Spirit effects and sustains the living process and brings creation towards the fulfilment of God's purposes. The Spirit remains creatively active in the world.

■ **Genesis :1-2; 2:4-7; Psalm 104:29-30; Romans 8:18-25**

In re-creation

The Holy Spirit is also the agent in the re-creation of God's people. This is the witness of the entire Bible, which is itself inspired by the Spirit. In Old Testament times, the Holy Spirit spoke through special messengers who were gifted for particular tasks. The later prophets, especially Joel, foretold the outpouring of God's Spirit on all people, a prophecy that was fulfilled at the Pentecost recorded in Acts 2. The prophet Isaiah foretold the coming of one in whom the Spirit of the Lord would dwell perfectly.

■ **Judges 6:34; 1 Samuel 10:10-11; Isaiah 11:1-5; Joel 2:28-32; Acts 2:14-36; 1 Corinthians 2:9-16; 2 Peter 1:20-21**

The Holy Spirit was active in the Incarnation: by his power God's Son was born of a woman. The Spirit was at work in the life and ministry of Jesus and in the mighty act of God that commenced the new creation by raising Jesus Christ from the dead.

■ **Luke 1:35; 3:21-22; 4:16-21; 1 Corinthians 2:9-16; 2 Peter 1:20-21**

The Holy Spirit convicts us of our sinfulness and need of salvation, and leads us to repentance and faith. Through regeneration, he imparts new life in Christ and enables us to live as saints in the reality of the Resurrection. He sanctifies us as God's people, enabling us to bear the fruit of the Spirit. He calls us to continual repentance. He re-awakens us to the memory of Jesus and continues to remind us that we are at present sinners saved by grace to live victoriously.

The Spirit enlightens and empowers us in the spiritual warfare of this present age. We are engaged in conflict with the principalities and powers of evil. These seek to overthrow the Kingdom of God, corrupt the Church and thwart its mission to evangelise and make Christian disciples.

We need not be oppressed by, nor preoccupied with, the demonic or the powers of darkness. 'The one who is in you is greater than the one who is in the world' (1 John 4:4). 'Put on the full armour of God so that you can take your stand against the devil's schemes' (Ephesians 6:11). We can rejoice in our hope of the eventual victorious completion of the struggle against the powers of darkness. (*See appendix 6.*)

■ **John 16:7-11; 1 Corinthians 6:11; Galatians 5:16-18; Ephesians 6:10-18; 1 John 4:1-6; 5:4-5**

The Holy Spirit intercedes for us and gives voice to our prayers, interpreting our unspoken needs at the throne of grace where Jesus Christ represents us before the Father.

The Holy Spirit gives wise counsel. As the Counsellor promised by Jesus, he comes alongside to help, witnessing Christ and bringing to the minds of his followers his precious example, teaching and love. He bestows understanding of our task, equipment for service and empowerment for mission.

■ **John 14:25-26; Romans 8:26-27**

The Holy Spirit indwells the believer. He imparts strength, peace, joy and courage to witness, enabling us to live holy lives. (*See chapters 8 and 9.*)

■ **John 16; Ephesians 3:14-19**

In the Church

At Pentecost the Holy Spirit became the creator of the Church through which God initiated the reign of Christ and the mission of his people. In the ongoing life of the Church the Spirit initiates and seeks to guide and sustain genuine religious revival and spiritual renewal. (*See chapter 10.*)

- ◆ He releases and directs new life in the Church.
- ◆ He creates fellowship.
- ◆ He inspires sacrificial love.

- ◆ He imparts humility.
- ◆ He endues believers with spiritual gifts. (*See appendix 8.*)

A mission empowered

The Holy Spirit is always contemporary. He is God acting for us today, giving us confidence in the Christian mission and enabling us to look forward with hope to the ultimate fulfilment of God's purposes. By pointing back to the work of Christ for us, he points ever forward to the Father's ultimate creative purpose of uniting all things in him.

Within the flow of the salvation story, the Holy Spirit, giver of life, guides and vitalizes our mission to live the story, to tell the story and to help others to make it their own. (*See chapter 10.*)

■ **Acts 1 and 2; 1 Corinthians 12:4; Ephesians 1:3-14**

A summary

> *We believe in God the Holy Spirit, Lord and giver of life, who convicts, regenerates, sanctifies and empowers for ministry all who believe in Christ as Saviour and Lord.*

Appendix 6

Spiritual warfare

'We believe that we are engaged in constant spiritual warfare with the principalities and powers of evil, who are seeking to overthrow the Church and frustrate its task of world evangelisation. We know our need to equip ourselves with God's armour and to fight this battle with the spiritual weapons of truth and prayer. For we detect the activity of our enemy, not only in false ideologies outside the Church, but also inside it in false gospels which twist Scripture and put people in the place of God. We need both watchfulness and discernment to safeguard the biblical gospel' (International Congress of World Evangelisation, Lausanne, Switzerland, July 1974, copyright Lausanne Committee for World Evangelisation, used by permission).

To protect the integrity of this commitment, we should test all teaching about spiritual warfare by the following criteria:

◆ Does it do justice to God as Father, Son and Holy Spirit – not one to the exclusion of the others?

◆ Does it avoid promoting a dualism of equal kingdoms of darkness and light?

◆ Does it obscure human responsibility before God?

◆ Does it side-track our evangelistic ministry?

◆ Does it uphold a communal understanding of the Kingdom of God?

◆ Does it agree with biblical concepts of human nature?

◆ Does it cohere with a theology of the Cross which calls to self-denial and to a Christian response to the mystery of suffering?

◆ Is it consistent with the total witness of Scripture and above all with the life and teaching of Jesus Christ?

■ **2 Corinthians 10:3-5; Ephesians 6:11-12; 1 John 4:1-6**

CHAPTER SIX

Distorted image

The doctrine of humanity

Related Doctrines

We believe that our first parents were created in a state of innocency, but by their disobedience they lost their purity and happiness, and that in consequence of their fall all men have become sinners, totally depraved, and as such are justly exposed to the wrath of God.

Christians believe that the arrival of human beings on the earth did not happen accidentally, but according to the deliberate purpose of God. Human life is sacred because we have been created, that is, brought into being, as the crown of God's creative activity, to love, worship, serve and enjoy him for ever.

However, to speak of the nobility of our creation is also to be made aware of the shameful reality of our sinfulness. From the Bible we learn that human beings were created by God in his own image. God's intention was that we would live in a state of love and harmony with him, and with one another, and with the rest of creation. He also made us free, wanting us to love him voluntarily, not as puppets. That freedom was, and is, misused, which accounts for the pain and paradox of our condition. The universal experience of human sin has brought estrangement from God and disharmony within God's created world. We therefore live in a state of confusion and distress and are unable of ourselves to fulfil the high purpose for which God created us, a situation which the Bible describes as a bondage to sin, resulting in spiritual death.

■ **Romans 6:16-23**

Creation and Fall: the biblical witness

This revelation, that we are both specially created and wilfully fallen, is discerned throughout Scripture. However, the first four chapters of Genesis are a key to understanding our human situation and the salvation story which subsequently unfolds. Much of what follows will be a commentary on these chapters.

In these chapters, we find the following truths.

- ◆ All humanity is created in the image of God.

- ◆ God's intention is the harmony of humanity with himself and all creation.

- ◆ We have been terribly scarred by sin arising from human disobedience.

- ◆ The consequence of sin is separation from God.

- ◆ This is our universal human condition.

■ **Genesis 1-4; Isaiah 43:27-28; 64:6; Jeremiah 2:20-21; John 3:19-21; Romans 5:12-14; 1 John 1:8**

Created in the image of God

This phrase captures all that Christians believe about the creation of human beings and their significant resemblance and relationship to the Creator. Male and female, we are made in God's image, so that we can enter into full fellowship with him and with one another.

God is free, personal spirit and this is mirrored in the gift of human personality. We are living beings with individuality, autonomy and reason. At the same time we long for deep spiritual communion with God.

Our capacity for human relationships reflects the tri-unity and steadfast love of God. This capacity finds an important expression in the family, and in the Church, when loving and responsible relationships are based on the making and keeping of covenants.

The creator God has also placed his mark upon us in our potential for creativity and our ability to appreciate beauty. The image of God is reflected in our awareness of the working of conscience, and is expressed in the possibility of holiness of character through God's sanctifying work in our lives.

God's intention for us all, as created in his image, has been realised in Jesus Christ. In him we see the full human expression of God's holiness and love. He is the one true image of God, the one through whom we find our hope of fulfilling God's intention.

We were created to live in harmony with God and the rest of creation, and 'in the beginning' did enjoy this innocence and purity. We were created to love, serve and enjoy God; to stand in a unique position within creation and before God as his stewards, responsible to him. We were created to mould, develop and care for all that God has made on earth.

■ **Genesis 1:26-31; 8:20-9:7; Psalm 8:4-8; Matthew 5:48; John 4:24; Romans 2:14-15; 8:29; Ephesians 4:24; James 3:9**

Fallen humanity

It is self-evident that, as we are, we have fallen very far from God's intention. Though made in God's image, we are marred and flawed by sin. This has caused disharmony throughout the whole created order. Not only are we ill at ease throughout the whole of our human personality, but also we are out of harmony with the created universe. We are at war with ourselves and with each other, between the sexes, and amongst races and cultures. Aware of inner strife and fearful of judgement, we turn away from God. This evil that troubles us is found not only in individual lives but also is built into the very structure of society. We are caught in its trap.

■ **Psalm 14:1-3; Romans 8:19-22**

The origin of sin

Sin is an intrusion into human life. It was not originally present in human nature. Our slavery to sin originated in human disobedience to God's command. In consequence, evil was known because sin was committed; and because the good was lost it was recognised and longed for.

Adam and Eve were tempted to usurp God's lordship. Their sin resulted from assenting to beguiling temptations, but it was human will which chose to disobey. The role of Satan indicates the pervasiveness and power of evil in our world, though it does not absolve us from our responsibility for sin.

■ **Genesis 3:1-7; Romans 1:18-32**

The nature of sin

Sin is failure to believe and trust in God, and so to desire to be independent of him. God gives commands and establishes moral laws for our good. In the Genesis account, the serpent at first undermined belief in God's commands, so preparing

61

Adam and Eve for disobedience. It is sin to act, as they did, in unbelief and to fail to trust God's goodness. To do so is to base our lives on a lie.

Sin is idolatry. The serpent assured Adam and Eve that rebellion would elevate them to a position of equality with God. Such rebellion represents a presumptuous attempt to place ourselves and our own will in the place of God. It is an attempt to attain abundant life by following the path of self-will. The result is that, far from rising into a state of godlike independence, we decline into a condition of spiritual slavery and moral destitution.

Sin is failure to live according to the high standard of love for God and one another that true humanity demands. Because our desires are corrupted by self-centredness, we miss the mark. We grieve God, a truth made starkly evident in the cross of Christ. We fail one another, not only by breaking rules, but also by violating the wholeness of persons and communities.

The common definition of sin as anything contrary to the known will of God can serve as a practical guide. Sin impairs our sense of what is right and our ability to discern God's will, though it rarely destroys it completely. Repeated acts of disobedience, together with the influence of a godless society and the blind acceptance of peer-group norms, may drastically deaden the conscience. This can result in a moral insensitivity that the New Testament describes as being 'dead in your transgressions and sins' (Ephesians 2:1). Only by the renewing power of the gospel can we hope to recover an awareness of God's will and the desire to do it.

Guilt feelings make us conscious of having sinned. Sometimes these feelings are excessive, brought about by pressure from others or problems of background or temperament. Genuine guilt is the result of conscious transgression and consequent blame: it arises from what we do.

Sin, however, relates to more than what we do. It arises from what we are. The doctrines of original sin and depravity address this truth.

■ **Genesis 6:5; Isaiah 14:12-20; 59:2-15; Mark 7:21-23; Romans 7:7-25; James 1:13-15; 4:17**

Original Sin

The term 'original sin' emphasises the origin and radical consequences of the Fall. It reminds us that, although originally an intrusion, sin is innate. Our tendency is to sin. In that sense, we are 'born in sin'. This does not refer to the physical aspects of procreation. Human instincts are morally neutral and can be used either creatively or destructively. The phrase 'born in sin' rather refers to our condition under the dominion of sin. We have been subject to an invasion of evil from which no one is exempted.

Depravity

The terms 'original sin' and 'depravity' are often used to mean the same thing, but the latter refers more specifically to the moral condition of fallen humanity, rather than to the beginnings of sin.

In statements of doctrine, depravity is often called total depravity. This does not mean that every person is as bad as he or she can be, but rather that the depravity which sin has produced in human nature extends to the total personality. No area of human nature remains unaffected.

We are sinful in disposition so that even attempts at righteousness are tainted with sin. Human freedom to respond to God and to make moral choices is therefore impaired. But God is gracious and through his indwelling Spirit, the inclination to sin can be overcome by the inclination to live according to the will and purpose of God.

■ **Psalm 51:1-5; Romans 5:12-15; 6:11-14; 1 Corinthians 15:21-22**

The consequence of sin

Separation from God

Sin leads to separation from God and loss of fellowship with him. In the story of the Fall, Adam and Eve disobey the command of God and give in to the temptation to sin. They seek to evade the Lord's presence, hiding from him among the trees of the garden. He calls out to them but their response to his seeking is fear.

Separation from God is the universal consequence of sin. Though God seeks us, and we are sometimes aware of his presence, there remains a separation caused by our disobedience, with resulting guilt and fear. Separated from God, the source of community, our relationships are threatened. Isolation and fragmentation destroy the fragile communion we have with one another and with the created world. This profound sense of isolation may stimulate a search for truth about the meaning of life. But only a desire to turn to him will result in an encounter with the living God.

For God's part, the consequence of sin is the punishment of the disobedient. In the Genesis narrative, Adam and Eve are banished from the garden where they have enjoyed God's presence and companionship. They experience the reality of the wrath of God.

■ **Genesis 3:8-24; Deuteronomy 4:26-31; Isaiah 59:2; Luke 16:19-31**

The wrath of God

Divine wrath is evidence of the faithfulness of God, who is righteous and true to himself. It is a powerful expression of the love and holiness of God. In his wrath, God judges and condemns sin, while in his love he seeks to bring us to repentance. In the book of Revelation, for example, it is the Lamb, embodying the saving love of God in Christ, who also expresses God's enduring wrath towards the impenitent. It is our own sin that brings the wrath of God upon us.

The wrath of God is purposeful and disciplinary at present, designed to lead us toward repentance. But although restrained now, in the final consummation that wrath will be complete when God's righteous judgement will be revealed to the ultimately unrepentant.

The Bible links our sinful state, our separation from God, and the wrath of God, with the sting or anguish of death. It also warns of the dreadful possibility of spiritual death resulting in final separation from God. To reject God's mercy is to risk becoming unable to respond to divine love. The consequence is that we die in sin.

■ **Psalm 5:4-8; Isaiah 48:9-11; John 3:36; 5:28-29; Romans 2:5-8; Revelation 5:6-10; 6:15-17**

Salvation through the grace of God

Scriptural revelation and our personal experience confirm the powerlessness of human nature to achieve moral reformation. Our only hope is in the grace of God which issues from God's will to overcome the separation caused by sin.

Because the divine image has been marred through sin, and because humanity now lives under the compulsion of sin, and because sin has caused separation from God, unaided human nature has been rendered powerless to achieve righteousness on its own. A saving relationship with God is not earned by good works. But what we cannot do for ourselves God has done for us as a work of divine grace.

■ **Jeremiah 29:12-13; 31:31-33; Mark 10:45; 2 Corinthians 5:18-19; Ephesians 2:1-10; 1 Thessalonians 5:9**

'At just the right time, when we were still powerless, Christ died for the ungodly.' 'For it is by grace you have been saved, through faith – and this is not from yourselves, it is the gift of God' (Romans 5:6; Ephesians 2:8).

A world to be saved

We look upon humanity not only as ruined by sin but also as ready for hope. The gospel story is infused with hope. It knows the story of sin's despair, but it plays out the drama of the triumph of grace. In mission, we are called to invite people to the drama – invite them to enter it, to let it become theirs, and then to rejoice as their own story takes the unexpected turn towards hope.

A summary

> *We believe that we were created in the image of God to live in harmony with God and creation, a state which was broken by disobedience and sin and, as a result, we live under the compulsion of sin, separated from God and unable to save ourselves.*

CHAPTER SEVEN

Salvation story

The doctrine of the Atonement

Related Doctrines

We believe that the Lord Jesus Christ has by His suffering and death made an atonement for the whole world so that whosoever will may be saved.

We believe that repentance towards God, faith in our Lord Jesus Christ and regeneration by the Holy Spirit, are necessary to salvation.

The cross of Jesus Christ stands at the very heart of the Christian faith. It is the greatest revelation of the love of God. Through the cross, God overcame the separation caused by sin. Once and for all, Jesus' death and resurrection opened the way for humanity to be reconciled to a loving God. This reconciliation is called the atonement, literally making at one, or 'at-one-ment'.

God has taken the initiative in providing the way. It remains with us to respond to the divine provision in repentance and faith in order to experience the personal benefit of reconciliation to God and fellowship with him.

The Atonement foreshadowed

The writings of the Old Testament are the first powerful witness that God is the author of our salvation. He is the God who saves. This theme is woven into the story of his relationship with his people from the beginning. If the story of the Fall describes the separation from God caused by sin, the Old Testament moves very swiftly to offer hope through God's gracious intervention.

In the book of Genesis, the rescue of Noah from the flood provided an example of God's saving activity. The call of Abraham signalled the making of a people committed to God by covenant and promise. Exodus is the book of redemption, for it describes the release of God's people from slavery in Egypt by the mighty act of God. By his covenant, the holy God provided a means of reconciliation for his sinful people. In spite of their sin, they could come to him. Through the system of sacrificial offerings that God had himself ordained, the covenant relationship was maintained.

The Old Testament revelation comes to a climax in the messages of the prophets. Many of them spoke clearly of a coming day when God would act definitively to deal with sin and bring peace to his people. They spoke of the transformation of the heart through a new, inward relationship and a new, redeemed community. Some began to look forward to the coming of God's Messiah who would inaugurate a new age of peace and justice.

The New Testament records that Jesus fulfilled his mission as Saviour and Messiah that was both prophesied and defined in the Scriptures of the Old Testament. He taught his disciples to find in Hebrew prophecy the key to unlocking the meaning of his death. Consequently the first Christians used texts from the Old Testament to confirm the validity of their message that the risen Jesus was both Lord and Christ.

■ **Exodus 6:6-8; Isaiah 9:6-7; 35:3-4; 53:4-6; Jeremiah 31:31-34; 33:14-16; Luke 24:25-27; Acts 8:32-35**

The Atonement completed

The reconciliation prophesied in the Old Testament was fulfilled in Christ. God took the initiative leading to our salvation. A Saviour was born who was Christ the Lord.

The divine initiative found its complete expression in the self-offering of Jesus Christ on the cross of Calvary. Fully open to God in life, he was fully obedient in death and laid down his life for others. By dying on the cross, Jesus made the atonement. The coming together of the Father's dynamic gift and the Son's loving response bridged the separation between ourselves and God. We are reconciled to God in Christ and our sins are forgiven.

Understanding the Atonement

There is no single comprehensive way to interpret the atonement through the sacrifice of Christ. But in the New Testament, helpful pictures, when taken together, provide insight into its meaning.

Jesus himself indicated that he had come as a redeemer to give his life as a *ransom*. The term 'ransom' was used in the slave markets of the ancient world where a slave was set free through the payment, by another, of a redemptive price. This picture illustrates our captivity to sin. It shows there is a price to be paid if captives to sin are to be set free. Our redemption is costly.

■ **Mark 10:45**

Another concept was borrowed from the law courts: anyone who breaks the law which is given for our good deserves punishment. Sin has consequences in God's morally ordered world. Jesus paid the penalty and bore the consequence of sin on our behalf: 'He was pierced for our transgressions, he was crushed for our iniquities' (Isaiah 53:5). Christ voluntarily accepted punishment as a *substitute* for us.

■ **John 10:11-18; 15:13; 2 Corinthians 5:21; 1 Peter 2:24**

Other New Testament pictures of the atonement emphasise that Christ became our once-and-for-all redemptive *sacrifice*. He gave himself for our sins and so fulfilled the purpose of the great sacrifices of the Hebrew faith, to restore fellowship. The shed blood of Christ provides a way by which all people can be reconciled to God. His was a vicarious sacrifice, one made on behalf of another. It was not made for his own personal sin, for he had none: it was made for us.

■ **Luke 22:19-20; Romans 3:25-26; Hebrews 9:12; 10:9-14**

The New Testament describes Christ's sacrifice as a *victory* over sin and over the powers of evil which imprison humanity. By our faith in what he has done for us we participate in the achievement of Christ's sacrifice. The Cross, the place of defeat, is the place of triumph. Christ's victory on the cross becomes our victory.

■ **Colossians 2:13-15**

The cross of Jesus is at the heart of the reconciling work of God. It is also in itself the most effective picture of *self-giving love*. We can be drawn to it or repelled by it but when acknowledged, few can remain indifferent to the God it reveals.

It is a call to be reconciled to the God of the Cross, and to love as he loved us.

■ **Romans 5:8**

Our atonement is made possible at the great cost of the sacrifice of Christ. 'God so loved the world that he gave his one and only Son, that whoever believes in him shall not perish but have eternal life' (John 3:16). Christ did for us what we could not do for ourselves. He embraced our sin that we might embrace his righteousness.

Our crucified and risen Lord

It is through the death of Jesus that our sins are forgiven and we are reconciled to God. The resurrection of Jesus Christ from death is the ultimate confirmation of God's work of salvation through him. The resurrection is God's great life-affirming act which transcends the boundary between life and death. God's creative power at work here reveals his glory and greatness. In his resurrection Jesus Christ passed through death to a new life in which he reigns with God the Father in Heaven. By the Resurrection his people are led to worship him as Lord and follow him into eternal life.

For that reason the Resurrection provides the triumphant climax to the gospel proclamation of the earliest Christians. The obedient self-giving of Jesus has opened the way to his exaltation and to our salvation.

■ **Acts 2:32-36; 1 Corinthians 15:3-4; Ephesians 1:19b-21; Philippians 2:6-11**

Death and life for all believers

By the death and resurrection of Jesus Christians enter into the new relationship with God that is described as 'the new creation'. New life begins when we participate in spirit in this great act of God. To turn away from our sinful life and to come to Christ in repentance and faith is to experience a kind of death. We are called to the same obedience to God and letting go of self that led Jesus to the cross.

When we put our faith in Christ we come into new life by receiving the Holy Spirit. Resurrection is not only something that happened to Jesus Christ, it is also, very powerfully, something that happens to his followers. In Christ, all of us can experience power over the twin enemies of sin and death. We will all die physically, but that ultimate death, which is the consequence of sin, has no more power over us. When we turn to Christ we begin immediately to be part of the new humanity that has been brought into being through his death and resurrection. Because of our fallen human condition, the new life cannot be experienced in its entirety now, but the risen Christ is our hope for the future, guaranteed by the living presence of the Holy Spirit in us.

■ **Acts 2:38; Romans 6:1-11; 1 Corinthians 15:14-18; 2 Corinthians 5:17; Hebrews 2:14-16; 1 John 3:2**

Grace and free will

The atonement is God's act of unconditional love for all people everywhere. All who receive Christ in faith, all who bear witness to Jesus Christ as Lord, pass from death into life and enter a new relationship with God through his grace. The doctrine of the atonement clearly reveals that God's grace is the basis of our salvation.

God is constantly at work by his grace to draw all people to himself. And yet response to God's grace is an act in which we ourselves are involved, in that we have been given free will and can accept or reject the new life that is offered to us.

Grace and free will are not easily harmonised, and this has led some Christians so to emphasise the grace and sovereignty of God as to teach a doctrine of predestination that disallows free will. Such a doctrine implies that God alone determines who will be saved without the need for any co-operative response from us. Free will, in this case, is undermined. On the other hand, it is possible to forget that our God-given free will is itself flawed by sin. It cannot operate in true freedom without the grace of God.

We believe that God destines to salvation all who believe in Jesus Christ. Without the grace and mercy of God, we have no hope. But it is possible for grace to be resisted or abandoned. The grace of God does not compromise the freedom God himself has given.

The love of God is such that, with profound sorrow, he allows us to reject him.

■ **Luke 15:11-31; John 3:14-16; 5:24; 12:32; Romans 10:9; 2 Corinthians 5:14-15; 1 Timothy 2:3-6; 2 Peter 3:9**

Repentance and faith

If we are to experience personally the saving effects of the atonement, we must respond to the grace of God as revealed in Christ's sacrificial act. That response is repentance and faith, which are linked together so as to be twin elements of one action. They are porch and door at the entrance to life in Christ. They may be distinct or woven into one experience, but each is indispensible and neither is possible without the accompanying grace of God.

Our repentance is a gift of grace through the Holy Spirit. Although often accompanied by sorrow, it is essentially joyful, not morbid, because it is our reponse to the good news of salvation. The Spirit stimulates within us a desire for a change of direction. We become more aware of our sinfulness and this moves us, not down into despair, but upward towards God. We long to turn away from our selfishness and sin and towards the self-giving love of God. We are drawn to confess our sins, renounce selfish life-styles and to make restitution for the sins of the past.

True repentance, however, must always be accompanied by faith in Christ. We can be sorry for acts of transgression and want to leave them behind. We can bear deep guilt over past sins and want to have our conscience cleansed. We can even make a major change and turn in a new direction. All this may be called repentance, but it is not the repentance that leads to life in Christ. Salvation results only when repentance is combined with faith in Christ as saviour.

Faith is focused on Jesus the Christ, the full expression of God's grace and mercy. Faith sees the crucified Jesus and is assured of forgiving grace. Faith sees the resurrected Jesus and is assured of life-changing grace. Sorrow for sins is profoundly deepened when we see Jesus through the eyes of faith. Our change of purpose and direction is given substance when in faith we see the obedient and self-giving Christ and decide to call him Lord. Faith transforms the longing for change into genuine repentance that sees the Christ, experiences his forgiveness and follows him unconditionally.

The outcome is justification. We are justified by grace through faith alone. Such faith is not just an assent to the truth of Scripture, but involves a trusting acceptance of God's grace in Christ and confidence in a pardoning God. By faith we know that God in Christ loves us and has given himself for us, and that we are reconciled to God by the blood of Christ. This is the joyful experience of those who are saved. This is the essence of the scriptural truth that we are justified by grace through faith alone. (*See chapter 8.*)

■ Jeremiah 31:18-19; Matthew 3:1-10; 21:32; Luke 13:1-5; John 3:21; 16:8-10; Acts 16:31; Romans 4:1-5, 16

A gospel to be proclaimed

The love and mercy of God are mysteries beyond human comprehension. In the story of our salvation we recognise the astounding generosity of God's love towards us and all people. We realise the depth and gravity of our sin and discover the joy of our salvation in Christ.

The Church's mission is to share the story of this generosity, to lift up the atoning Cross for all the world to see, to proclaim the gospel's inclusiveness, to demonstrate its saving power, and to pray urgently that people everywhere will know the grace of our Lord Jesus Christ.

A summary

We believe that the Lord Jesus Christ suffered and died to save the whole world and was raised by the glory of the Father so that whoever turns in repentance to God and has faith in Jesus Christ will be saved.

CHAPTER EIGHT

Salvation experience

The doctrine of salvation

Related Doctrines

We believe that repentance towards God, faith in our Lord Jesus Christ, and regeneration by the Holy Spirit, are necessary to salvation.

We believe that we are justified by grace through faith in our Lord Jesus Christ and that he that believeth hath the witness in himself.

We believe that continuance in a state of salvation depends upon continued obedient faith in Christ.

This chapter is concerned first and foremost with our personal experience of salvation. If the transforming grace brought about by the atonement is to save us, we must appropriate the universal work of Christ on the cross for ourselves. This comes about, not by understanding the doctrine, but by trusting in the one who saves. Therefore we consider the blessings received when, by our response to God's grace, Christ becomes alive in us.

Those who come to God in true repentance and faith discover the overwhelming reality of his freely offered forgiveness. The result is a transformation of life, a revolution that can only be described as a new creation.

The blessings of salvation

The word generally used to describe becoming a Christian is the word conversion. It indicates a change of direction, an about-turn, a change of heart. It means entering into a new relationship with God in which unbelief is replaced by humble trust, resulting in new life.

This new relationship brings with it great joy and many blessings. There is open communication between ourselves and God: the pain of separation is past. We are aware of new desires for good and new power to realise them. We enjoy a sense of confidence in God's presence and feel ourselves to be part of a new family. We long for more of God and his reality in our present and our future. Such blessings as these have been expressed in the language of Christian doctrine, for example: justification, regeneration, assurance, adoption and sanctification. The terms are important in identifying the nature of our personal experience and grounding it in the universal experience of Christian believers.

Justification

The word justification describes the act of God for us which changes the relationship between ourselves and him. Although we are sinners, God declares us righteous because of our faith in Jesus Christ. We are accepted by God just as we are. We do not deserve such acceptance, neither can we earn it, or repay it. We can only experience the joy of forgiveness and open communion with God. Like the returning prodigal in Jesus' parable, we are treated as those who have the right to the Father's fellowship and esteem. We know ourselves to be children of God, and are affirmed in our relationship with him and with one another. We are fully adopted into the family of God.

Our justification depends upon the character of God, the saving work of Jesus Christ and our faith in him. God, who is righteous, merciful and true, has reached out in the person of Jesus Christ to save the guilty and helpless. We are acquitted of our sin, accepted by God and our sins are forgiven because God is gracious and merciful. This is the gift of God.

Jesus taught the gracious fatherhood of God and the need for humble faith in his mercy. Much of Paul's teaching concerned justification, God's way of restoring all people to a right relationship with himself through faith in Christ. Justification is central to the good news of the gospel.

■ **Luke 15:17-24; 18:9-14; Romans 1:17; 3:21-26; 8:15-17; Galatians 4:3-7; Ephesians 1:3-12; Titus 3:4-7**

Justified by grace

God seeks us before we even desire to seek him. His grace is totally unmerited, a characteristic of God's dealings with us at all times, seen supremely in the love and compassion of Jesus Christ. It awakens us, convicts us of sin, convinces us of hope, enables us to respond and leads to new life.

We cannot, however, presume upon God's forgiveness. He does not provide a general amnesty for unrepentant sinners. It is by his grace that we are awakened to our need of salvation.

The term 'prevenient grace', the grace that comes before conversion, describes this preparatory work of the Holy Spirit. Our moral sense, or conscience, though imperfect because of ignorance and sin, can act as a stimulus to spiritual awakening. God gives a measure of moral enlightenment to us all, and the teaching of Jesus assures us that those who hunger and thirst for righteousness will be satisfied. All this is a work of the Spirit who can transform such natural remorse or human moral philosophy into a true awareness of God.

It is through the grace of God that the Holy Spirit convicts of sin. He reveals our real guilt as opposed to feelings aroused by cultural or religious factors or excessive introspection. Grace that leads to this conviction has positive results – repentance, forgiveness and new life.

From first to last, our justification is by the grace of God. It is the grace of God that saves us when we first exercise justifying faith. Life in Christ demands continual reliance on the grace of God, and not on our own goodness to earn God's favour. We are always in God's debt, always undeserving, always accepted by grace alone. God's saving grace will be complete only when our infirmities are finally removed and our bodies are transformed with the dawn of resurrection.

■ **Hosea 11:3-4, 8-9; John 1:9-18; Romans 1:19-23; 5:8; Ephesians 2:4-10**

Justification through faith

Faith is our personal response to the grace of God. It is a trusting acceptance of the good news of the gospel, that God accepts us because of Jesus Christ. It involves a commitment of ourselves to him, an obedient response to his goodness and a desire to follow him in the way of discipleship.

Therefore, faith is more than intellectual belief. Though faith in Christ requires the use of our minds, it is possible to assent to a creed without trusting the Saviour. Justifying faith involves heart, mind and will, and is made possible by God himself who bestows faith on those who desire it.

Faith in itself is not a good work, although genuine Christian faith issues in good works. It is not a human achievement that wins or earns reward. It is the God-given channel through which grace flows. It is an attitude rather than an action.

Those who attempt to win acceptance with God by their own performance are doomed to continual frustration and unease because the greatest human effort can never fulfil all the requirements of true righteousness. Even if our outward lives appear to be flawless in conduct, we know that our thoughts and motives fall short of pleasing God. Greater striving may make us more self-centred and less God-directed, more judgmental and self-absorbed. A host of good works cannot build up a credit balance in God's accounting nor outweigh our sin.

But when we abandon human efforts and cast ourselves in repentance on the merciful grace of God, his grace is freely given. We are freed from guilt and accepted as righteous in and through Jesus Christ. Then, confidently resting on God's mercy, we discover the new way of righteousness, based not on human striving but on the life-giving grace of God.

■ **Psalm 37:3-6; 103:4-8; John 6:28-29; Acts 13:39; Romans 4:16; 5:1-2**

Regeneration

The essence of justification by faith is that we are accepted by God as we are. Although we are sinners, our faith in Christ's atonement leads to forgiveness and hope. We know that God is for us in Jesus. This tremendous change in our relationship with God brings to life new desires for inward purity and love for others. These desires are signs of the experience of new life, the spiritual transformation that we call regeneration.

The blessing of regeneration is described in the New Testament in a number of ways. In the Gospel of John, Jesus speaks of the need for those who would see the Kingdom of God to be born again. He is describing the rebirth in the Spirit that comes about through faith. Paul uses the idea of new creation to illustrate the death of the old life and the beginning of the new. The language indicates an inward revolution as well as an outward change in our status before God. The gift of the Holy Spirit is new life.

Regeneration is wedded to justification. It is distinct from justification but closely related to it, and the two are inseparable in our own experience. Justification is God's work for us, the forgiveness of our sins and our change of status before God. It does not depend on our moral renewal. Regeneration is God's work in us, the gift of the indwelling Spirit and the beginning of a life of holiness. It is our call to the Christlike life and does involve our moral renewal.

Regeneration means that we die to our old life and come alive to Christ. We are alive to the presence of Christ with us, we hear his call to follow him and we experience his peace and joy in our hearts. We are sensitive to sin and eager to seek forgiveness. The fruit of the Spirit becomes evident in us as a visible sign of regeneration. The Spirit guides us as we reach out to share the love of God with others. We look to the future rather than the past and are filled with hope. We learn to grow in the knowledge and love of Jesus Christ. This regeneration is the first step in a life of holiness in Christ.

It is helpful to recognise that there is a paradox in our relationship with God that the twin blessings of justification and regeneration address. Justification speaks of a decisive change in our relationship with God through faith in Christ, from alienation to acceptance. Regeneration speaks of the life of the Spirit imparted to us, the ongoing work of grace in our lives in which we must co-operate. We know both the joy and the pain of the growth to which true righteousness invites us. Both regeneration and justification are true: though God calls us on to holiness of life, he always accepts us as his children and through the Spirit reassures us of our place with him.

■ **John 3:3-8; Romans 6:1-5; 2 Corinthians 5:17; Titus 3:3-7**

Assurance

We believe that God, who has accepted and saved us and given us eternal life, has given us also the assurance of our standing in him. The Holy Spirit is the seal and guarantee of our salvation and assures us of the truth of the gospel message and its effectiveness for us. Our new life, our determination to obey God, our break with the past and our new spiritual direction give evidence of our *adoption* into God's family. We can be assured because the Holy Spirit speaks to us and our lives have been changed.

Our confidence is based not on changing moods or feelings but on the word of God. When we accept the biblical promises of God concerning our justification and regeneration, and our acceptance into God's family, we base our trust on the faithfulness of God who has given his promise and who can be trusted.

Assurance does not mean that we may never be troubled by doubt following our conversion or that we shall always be consciously aware of the work of the Spirit within us. At times when we are not conciously assured of our salvation, however, we remember that an ongoing union with Christ depends on his work and not our feelings.

Some people receive their *assurance* in a moment of intense experience; with others the assurance is quietly given like the slow breaking of the dawn. Such assurance must be affirmed daily by obedience and never made an excuse for carelessness or complacent presumption. It is the changed life that is evidence for the work of grace within.

It is God's will that his children should know they belong to his family and so continue on their way in joyful confidence, not in fearful uncertainty. The gospel call to salvation is to faith, not fear.

■ **Psalm 138:7-8; Romans 8:14-17, 35-39; 2 Corinthians 13:5-7; Ephesians 1:13-14; Philippians 1:6; 1 John 4:19-24; 5:10**

Backsliding

Assurance does not mean that our salvation is guaranteed to us against our own free will. It is possible to cease to obey Christ and so to forfeit our hope of eternal life. This is consistent with our understanding of the grace of God, who always leaves us open to respond freely to him. Freedom to live by grace includes freedom to turn away.

Backsliding, then, is possible for true Christians. It can occur through the deliberate rejection of Christ, or, more insidiously, when we drift from the way of discipleship or neglect the means of grace. This does not mean that every time we sin we slide away from the grace of God. Even our many failures will not deprive us of the Holy Spirit's presence if we turn to him for forgiveness and restoration.

When we live a life of continued obedient faith in Christ we need not fall from grace and be eternally lost. This life involves the spiritual disciplines of prayer, Bible study, and self-denial, as well as openness to the ministry of the body of Christ through worship, teaching, caring and service.

To develop and nurture a life secured by a total trust in God's grace, we should not be daunted by the possibility of being tempted beyond our powers. Our obedient faith, which enabled us to know Christ as saviour, will not be sustained by over-anxiety about staying saved, or by limiting our involvement with life for fear of backsliding. Our faith will be assured as in obedience to Christ's call to serve we keep close to him: to risk our lives wherever there is human need, challenge sin and dare to live the Christian life in all its fullness.

■ **John 15:1-6; 1 Corinthians 10:6-13; Hebrews 2:1-3; 6:4-6; 10:19-39; Jude 20-21; Revelation 2:4-5; 3:1-6, 14-22**

A salvation to be claimed

The mission of the Church is to invite the world to claim this salvation. The Church that has received the good news of grace has the privilege of preaching it to a world in despair. The Church that has learned to trust in Jesus has the joy of inviting to faith those who no longer trust. The Church that has the assurance of sins forgiven has the confidence to bring this message of God's reliable provision.

A summary

> *We believe that we are justified by grace through faith in our Lord Jesus Christ, and are born again by the Holy Spirit, who testifies to salvation in our hearts as we continue in an obedient faith-relationship with Christ.*

CHAPTER NINE

Full salvation

The doctrine of holiness

Related Doctrines

We believe that continuance in a state of salvation depends upon continued obedient faith in Christ.

We believe that it is the privilege of all believers to be wholly sanctified, and that their whole spirit and soul and body may be preserved blameless unto the coming of our Lord Jesus Christ.

God's purpose in saving us is to create in us the likeness of his Son, Jesus Christ, who is the true image of God. It is to impart the holiness of Jesus so that we may 'participate in the divine nature' (2 Peter 1:4). It is to make it possible for us to glorify God as Christ's true disciples. It is to make us holy.

Continued obedient faith

Our salvation is assured as long as we continue to exercise faith in Jesus Christ. Such faith is expressed in obedience to his leadings, will and commands. Obedience as a free-will choice is a consequence of faith, and without it, faith dies.

Our conversion inaugurates a journey during which we are being transformed into Christ's likeness. Thus salvation is neither a state to be preserved nor an insurance policy which requires no further investment. It is the beginning of a pilgrimage with Christ. This pilgrimage requires from us the obedience of separation from sin and consecration to the purposes of God. This is why 'obedient faith' is crucial: it makes pilgrimage possible.

Our Christian pilgrimage is a faith-journey inviting us to a life of discipleship. Through prayer and the study of God's word, we grow in communion with him. By following Christ we learn to put into practice what we hear through the Spirit. We grow in obedience and faithfulness to God. We begin to discover that obedient faith is given by God's grace, rather than achieved by our superlative efforts.

We become aware of the sanctifying work of the Holy Spirit.

■ **Matthew 6:9-10; 21:28-31; Colossians 2:6-7; 1 Thessalonians 5:12-22; 2 Thessalonians 2:13-14; Hebrews 10:26-36; 2 Peter 3:18; 1 John 5:1-5; Jude 20-21**

The sanctifying Spirit at work

With the liberating experience of salvation, comes the glory of the presence and living reality of the Holy Spirit which is a beginning to the life of holiness. This glory honours, blesses and also burdens us.

Our new freedom in Christ and the regenerating presence of the Holy Spirit make us more aware of the power of sin. Sometimes we can even know defeat, experience disillusionment and fall into disobedience. The result can be a feeling of powerlessness and sometimes personal guilt. We may withdraw from loving communion with the Holy Spirit, question our vision of the victorious life, and consequently abstain from the painful, challenging process of learning obedience and maturing as Christians. Even the purpose of our salvation may at times seem thwarted.

Sanctification by grace through faith is the answer to this dilemma. The terms 'sanctification, 'sanctify' and to be 'sanctified' are translations of the Hebrew and Greek words of Scripture used to describe the holiness of God and the action by which God's children are made holy and set apart for God's purposes. The King James Version of 1 Thessalonians 5:23 referred to in the tenth Salvation Army statement of faith particularly relates to this action of God: 'We believe that it is the privilege of all believers to be wholly sanctified, and that their whole spirit and soul and body may be preserved blameless unto the coming of our Lord Jesus Christ'.

Discovering and appropriating for ourselves the sanctifying power of the Holy Spirit is not a new experience unrelated to saving faith and the experience of regeneration. The same grace at work in our lives both saves and sanctifies. We advance towards the fulfilment of that which our conversion promises – victory over sin, the life of holiness made actual, and all of the graces of salvation imparted by the presence and action of the indwelling Holy Spirit and his sanctifying power.

God's gracious provision

By God's gracious provision we are not left alone with our defeat, disobedience and guilt. The Holy Spirit is at work in us and calls us to that holiness which is the privilege of all believers.

We are called to reflect the holiness of God. God is holy, awesome in his majesty and in the beauty of his character. He is all that true love could desire. His children are called to a related holiness, dedicated to the service of the holy God and called to be like him in character.

This is not a call directed to an elect few, nor to an elite who have particular spiritual qualifications. Nor does the phrase, 'the privilege of all believers' mean it is optional. It is God's intention for all his people. The call comes to us all: 'Be holy because I am holy' (1 Peter 1:16).

The life of holiness is not mysterious or overwhelming or too difficult to understand. It is life in the footsteps of Christ who is the true image of God. He is the truly holy one, who revealed the holiness of God in the wholeness and fullness of his human life and in the manner of his self-offering to God. To see him is to understand the nature of holiness, and to follow him is to be marked by it. Holiness is Christlikeness.

Holiness is the realisation of the Christ-life within us. It is the present purpose and positive benefit of our salvation. It is the renewal of our humanity according to the pattern or image of God our creator. The power of the sin that was cancelled on the Cross is now broken. Discipleship is now the life of the Christian.

This work of God makes it possible to live according to the purpose for which we were created: to enjoy the gifts of God, to serve and worship him through our living, and to share human fellowship in love and service. God sanctifies us so that we may share fellowship with him to his pleasure, live fulfilled human lives and carry out his mission in the world.

■ **John 17:15-19; Philippians 1:6; 1 Thessalonians 4:1-8; 5:23; 2 Thessalonians 2:13-14; 1 Peter 1:13-16**

By grace through faith

The sanctifying Spirit makes this experience possible. In regeneration, we receive the Holy Spirit who creates new life in Christ and fills us with joy and the assurance of salvation. The

Spirit then remains with us. His sanctifying work becomes a reality for us through the life of faith which involves both trust in and continued obedience towards God.

Even though the Holy Spirit is at work in our lives, he never imposes himself on us or undermines our freedom of choice. The desire for holiness must be in us, and the sincerity of this intention must be affirmed by dedicating our lives to Christ. As we act in faith, we experience sanctification. The possibility of holiness becomes a reality only through faith, by trusting the grace of the sanctifying God and obeying his word.

■ **John 3:6; Romans 8:1-11; 2 Corinthians 3:17-18; 7:1; Hebrews 12:12-14**

A radical life-change

The Cross is at the heart of the holiness experience. It points the way to a radical new life. Scripture describes in dramatic terms our decisive dying to the old self and to sin, as we identify with Christ in his death for us and recognise that in a profound sense we died in him.

God's sanctifying work is a life-changing experience whereby we are empowered to make radical changes of direction in our lives. Sometimes a compelling glimpse of the holiness of God opens our eyes to our need of purity. We may be stimulated to seek to live a holy life because we long for a more satisfying relationship with God. The call to service may lead to a deeper desire for sanctifying grace. We may experience the pain and agony of encountering evil and sin lurking within us. We may become aware of our inclination to give in to temptation or relax our guard. The Holy Spirit's leading and our own desire for more of God may in such circumstances lead to a spiritual crisis.

At such times the Holy Spirit is overwhelmingly present with power for holy living. We experience a moment of grace that leads to spiritual breakthrough. We move into a new level of relationship with the holy God, with others and with ourselves.

Such life-changing moments are widespread, but dramatic experiences are not always a feature of our growth in holiness. The Holy Spirit deals with us as individuals and leads us on into holiness in the way he sees fit.

We should judge the growth of our spiritual life not by the depth and intensity of our spiritual experiences so much as by the quality of our obedience.

■ **Romans 6:1-14; 12:1-2; 2 Corinthians 5:14-15; Galatians 2:20; Ephesians 3:14-19; Philippians 1:9-11; Colossians 3:5-14**

A lifelong process

There is a crisis/process dynamic in the life of holiness. Experienced as a crisis, sanctification becomes a lifelong process. We are in the process of becoming what we already are in Christ. The holy life, however, will always be marked by an 'already but not yet' reality. We are already sanctified but not yet sinlessly perfect.

Sanctification by the Holy Spirit can extend to the whole or entire personality with no area of life unaffected, just as the pervasive effects of sin have penetrated every area of human life. However, the doctrine of entire sanctification does not mean that in this life we ever arrive at a point where further spiritual progress is unnecessary for those sanctified, even as total depravity does not mean that each of the unredeemed is as bad as he or she can be.

The truly holy life is marked by the signature and seal of Christ himself. 'He anointed us, set his seal of ownership on us, and put his Spirit in our hearts as a deposit, guaranteeing what is to come' (2 Corinthians 1:21-22). In response, first and foremost we seek close communion with God, marked by openness and obedience to him. Out of this relationship is born the fruit of Christlikeness as we become more and more conformed to Christ and his holiness is imparted. This communion accords with our deepest longing and wish. Paul describes it as 'Christ living in me' (Galatians 2:20). We experience the presence of Christ, crucified and risen, in our own lives.

Christ's presence changes us as we live in and through him. Our self-image undergoes a change. We rest in the knowledge of the love, grace and acceptance of God and this sets us at peace and brings us self-acceptance.

As we follow Jesus, who came to seek and save the lost, we sense the call to serve others in Christ's name. We build relationships with the lost, the abused, the forgotten, the powerless. In them we see Christ. We are drawn to search for truth and justice and the righting of wrongs in the name of Christ.

The holy life is a sacramental life. Reflecting Jesus, it is an open and visible sign of the grace of God. It is a fulfilled human life, a life of close communion with God and self-forgetful service to others. It is a life that anticipates our final sanctification when we are glorified, as eternity breaks through and God becomes all in all.

■ **John 15:1-7; Galatians 5:16-25; Ephesians 4:13-15; 1 Thessalonians 3:11-13; 2 Peter 3:18; 1 John 3:1-3, 18-20**

The life of holiness

The restoration of the covenant

As the Fall resulted in the fragmentation of all relationships, so the restored image of God in us expresses itself in the renewal of our relationships. This restoration is crucial to holy living. Since God is a covenant-making and a covenant-keeping God, our relationships also have the character of covenant. This character means that our relationships, both with God and with others, are built on love and faithfulness.

In the Bible, the concept of covenant underlies all relationships. Righteousness is realised in a relationship of love within a covenant of obedience to God, care for others and faithfulness to moral values. Seeking to glorify God and value people, it pursues love within the God-given intention of the relationship.

We are first and foremost in covenant with God who faithfully keeps his covenant of love with us. As we respond to that love, our relationship with him deepens and we are drawn closer to him. As this love grows, it expresses itself in the life of discipleship. The sanctified believer is empowered by love and guided by obedience to keep covenant.

As our relationship with God unfolds, love for God draws us to the others whom God loves, and obedient discipleship motivates us to put love into action. Our participation in caring fellowship overcomes our selfishness, challenges our self-righteousness and leads us on to love, humility, wholeness and a desire to see others brought into covenant with God.

Our relationship with God's world is also transformed. We see the beauty and reflection of God in it and acknowledge that it is his world, the fruit of his creation. Hostility toward the created world disappears, and we come to understand our role as stewards.

Holiness, then, expresses itself socially in covenants. It both places us in the social arena and transforms our relationships.

Holiness and ethics

Ethics deals primarily with important relational issues. Holiness is true love, nurtured and expressed in relationships. For this reason, Christian ethics is an extremely important dimension and discipline of holy living. It provides the principles and guidelines for the fullness of love in all our relationships.

Jesus Christ is the fulfilment of all that the Old Testament law had promised and anticipated. He taught that the Law was, in fact, fulfilled in love. This was the ethic of love. To realise Jesus' radical ethic of love is to treat all our relationships as holy covenants. God is able to love through us. This transformation is what makes social holiness possible and what enables us to live by the radical ethic of love.

■ **Matthew 5:43-48; Mark 12:28-31; Luke 10:25-37; 1 John 4:7-21**

Wholeness, health and healing

The God who sanctifies is the healing God who makes us whole. The term 'wholeness' points to the comprehensiveness of God's saving work in Christ and of the Spirit's sanctification.

The Gospels reveal that Jesus cared about every dimension of human life and how sin has distorted it, and that his ministry demonstrated a healing response to human suffering and disease in all its forms. Again and again, the New Testament as a whole records the healing work of the Holy Spirit. The restoration of the covenant required the restoration of health in every relationship of human life: spiritual, emotional, social, physical.

This means that there is no holiness without wholeness. Holiness can only be seen as redemptively touching all of life. This does not mean, however, that those who are physically healthy, or emotionally stable, or socially adjusted, or economically prosperous are holy. Nor does it mean that those who suffer from physical infirmity, emotional turmoil, social maladjustment, or economic deprivation are thus sinful. What it does mean is that in claiming holiness we claim the promise of wholeness in all of life. The holy life is then the Spirit-led journey toward wholeness in Christ.

As Jesus refused to attribute illness to specific sin, so we see every form of disease or infirmity only as a manifestation of the overall human condition. And as he did not heal all diseases and restore every broken relationship, so we recognise that the sanctified do not manifest the signs of complete healing in every area of life. There is a wholeness in brokenness. The healing we rightfully claim is profound, the effects may await eternity.

As God's holy people we are concerned not only about our own wholeness and health but also about that of others. Thereby we who know healing for ourselves become a healing community engaged in a healing mission.

■ **Psalm 30:2; 103:3; Matthew 20:34; Mark 2:1-12; Luke 4:18; 7:22; John 9:3; 12:40; Acts 5:16; 10:38; 1 Corinthians 12:28; 2 Corinthians 5:16-21; Ephesians 2:11-22; James 5:13-16; 1 Peter 2:24; Revelation 22:1-2**

A holiness to be lived out in mission

The holy life is a Christ-service for the world, expressed through a healing, life-giving and loving ministry. It is the life of Christ which we live out in mission. God sanctifies his people not only in order that they will be marked by his character, but also in order that the world will be marked by that character. God changes the structures of society through a variety of means, but he changes them as well through the mission of his sanctified people, empowered and gifted by his Holy Spirit.

The mission of God's holy people encompasses evangelism, service and social action. It is the holy love of God, expressed in the heart and life of his people, pointing the world to Christ, inviting the world to saving grace, serving the world with Christ's compassion and attacking social evils. Holiness leads to mission.

A summary

We believe in sanctification by grace through faith as the privilege and calling of all who profess Jesus Christ as their Lord and Saviour and who accept the power of the Holy Spirit to lead a life of holiness.

Appendix 7

Interpretations of the holiness experience

The experience of holiness has been expressed in a number of different ways, none of which reveals the whole truth or full dimension of it. Among the most well known are the following.

The term *entire sanctification* is derived from 1 Thessalonians 5:23 (*KJV*). It expresses the belief that sanctification affects the whole personality and reaches the depths of the soul. The term should not be used, however, to suggest a state of sinless perfection. Rather, it means that we are whole or complete, and conscious that sinning is foreign to our new being in Christ. If we do commit sin, we acknowledge it honestly, confess it before God, make restitution and move on. Entire sanctification means that, while we abide in Christ, we are free from the power of sin to undermine, destroy or divide us. We are free to be what all of us are called to be. (See, for example, Romans 1:7, 'To all in Rome who are led by God and called to be saints'; and 2 Thessalonians 2:13-14.)

Full salvation refers to the completion of Christ's saving work in our hearts. At our conversion, we may not grasp the fullness nor claim the full benefit of what the atonement has made possible. Our attempts to live the Christian life may sometimes meet with failure. This failure may cause us to discover that saving grace is also sanctifying grace: that we can be cleansed from all sin, and that we can have victory and fulfilment as disciples of Jesus. We claim – and by the power of the Holy Spirit we experience – *full* salvation. The concept of full salvation, however, should not be understood as a state of spiritual saturation beyond which we cannot receive further grace. It simply refers to our faith in, and openness toward, the full gift of God's grace. A life founded on this full gift, and changed by its powerful content, is a holy life.

The *infilling*, or *fullness, of the Holy Spirit* is a phrase used to describe the fullness by which we are empowered to live the Christ-life and to be witnesses. As a result, the joy of the Lord expels and replaces defeatist attitudes. Holiness is fullness in the Spirit. In using the term 'infilling', care should be taken not to depersonalise God by likening him to fluid that can be poured into us as empty vessels. Furthermore, this, and other interpretations of the work of the Holy Spirit, should not be taken to mean that other persons of the Trinity are excluded. Rather, the term, 'infilling of the Holy Spirit' means that God himself comes in all his fullness by the agency of the person of the Holy Spirit.

The baptism of the Holy Spirit is a way some have used to describe the holiness experience. Baptism is a symbol of dying to ourselves and emerging as new persons in Christ. It was used in the Early Church as the receiving of the Holy Spirit at regeneration which was the requirement for membership in the body of Christ: 'We were all baptised by one Spirit into one body' (1 Corinthians 12:13). The 'baptism of the Holy Spirit' may therefore be considered as distinct from being 'filled with the Holy Spirit'. Baptism happens once at the beginning of Christian experience, while infilling happens repeatedly throughout the Christian life. In some usage, however, baptism and infilling are equated, with the phrase, 'the baptism of the Holy Spirit', suggesting a movement beyond forgiveness of sins to a Spirit-filled newness of life. We must be careful not to place Christian experiences into separate compartments. God's sanctifying power is no less a benefit and work of the same saving grace, whether appropriated in experience at conversion or subsequently.

The term *baptisms in the Spirit* has also been used to describe repeated experiences of infilling or endowments of spiritual power. The use of the term in both the singular and the plural sense has caused considerable confusion.

The term *second work of grace or second blessing* has been used in holiness movements, including The Salvation Army, to distinguish the experience of sanctification from the experience of justification and regeneration, following the teaching of John Wesley. We should be cautious about requiring for every Christian 'a second work of grace' that must be chronologically subsequent to the 'first work of grace'. The sanctifying grace of God is not limited to human timetables. In the experience of some, full salvation may come at conversion while for others it happens subsequently. A 'second blessing' does not imply that there are only two blessings, or that a second blessing is the final completion of Christian maturity and development. The Wesleyan doctrine of the second blessing relates however to actual experiences of a spiritual crisis subsequent to conversion. As a vision of the potential for all believers in Christ, it is a powerful means of encouraging all Christians to partake in the fullness of the grace of God.

Heart cleansing or the blessing of a clean heart is a term used to emphasise the removal of inbred sin and unworthy, self-centred attitudes of the mind and heart. 'Heart cleansing' implies that our motivation has been purified and all our actions are now driven by love. The concept of 'purity of motives', however, must be used with great care. Using 'purification of motives' as the basis, we may refuse to admit and confess any specific personal acts of sin: only 'mistakes' are admitted. Purity is a love-gift to which we open ourselves, and which we allow to claim us, but never use to our own advantage.

Perfect love is perhaps the most comprehensive description of holiness, although a description which can be simply expressed. Through his sanctifying power, the Holy Spirit fills us with God's perfect love, so that we begin to love, not with our own, seriously flawed love, but with the unselfish love of Christ. We are thereby equipped for the path of fulfilling Christ's commandment: 'Love the Lord your God with all your heart and with all your soul and with all your strength and with all your mind;' and, 'love your neighbour as yourself' (Luke 10:27).

Wrong paths

Sanctification does not mean the *elimination of* all possibility for *sinning*. Although it is possible through the Holy Spirit *not* to sin, even when we experience a fullness of God's sanctifying power there remains the *possibility* of sinning. There are still remnants of behaviour patterns which can recur. There is still the human tendency to give in to temptation.

In the same way, we must not claim *sinless perfection* in this life. Temptations will always be our companions in life, but by the Christ-forming power of the Holy Spirit in us, we can successfully resist temptations and not fall into sin. We cannot say, however, that sin is not a possibility for the sanctified.

On the other hand, neither can we say that those who experience a fullness of God's sanctifying power inevitably, sooner or later, fall into sin. Those who insist on the *sinful imperfection* of all believers fail to acknowledge the full benefit and work of the atonement. When we are born again of the Spirit we are no longer in bondage to sin: we are set free.

To insist that believers are necessarily sinful, or that they continue to be prone to personal sin, is to limit the power of the atonement to bring about a thorough change of character and a comprehensive victory over sin. We do not sin inevitably. We may sin, but when we do, we recognise that sin is contradictory and foreign to who we are in Christ. Then we confess it to God and to whomever we have wronged, and are renewed in grace.

CHAPTER TEN

People of God

The doctrine of the Church

'Of this Great Church of the Living God, we claim and have ever claimed, that we of The Salvation Army are an integral part and element – a living fruit-bearing branch in the True Vine.' (Bramwell Booth)

The Church is the fellowship of all who are justified and sanctified by grace through faith in Christ. Membership in the body of Christ is not optional for believers: it is a reality given to all who know Christ, the head of the Church. It is a benefit of the atonement through which we are invited into fellowship with God and with one another.

Salvation Army doctrine implies a doctrine of the Church. Each doctrine begins: 'We believe . . . .' 'We' points to a body of believers, a community of faith – a church.

One very important change since the Eleven Articles were formulated and adopted is the evolution of the Movement from an agency for evangelism to a church, an evangelistic body of believers who worship, fellowship, minister and are in mission together.

Salvationists are members of the one body of Christ. We share common ground with the universal Church while manifesting our own characteristics. As one particular expression of the Church, The Salvation Army participates with other Christian denominations and congregations in mission and ministry. We are part of the one, universal Church.

The corps is The Salvation Army's local congregation. It is a concrete expression of the Church. It has its own ways of worshipping, training and serving, based on the teaching of the Bible, the guidance of the Holy Spirit and the nature of its mission. But its purpose is consistent with the calling of the one, universal Church. Its three key strengths are its evangelistic zeal, its commitment to holiness and its strong community outreach.

The body of Christ

When we speak of the Church as the body of Christ we mean that all believers are incorporated in spiritual union with Christ their head, and with one another as fellow members working in harmony. We mean that the Church is Christ's visible presence in the world, given life by the indwelling of the Holy Spirit and called to grow in conformity to Christ.

Scripture teaches that every member of the body has an essential part to play if the whole is to function to the glory of God, and that without the presence and participation of every member, the body suffers.

■ **Romans 12:4-5; 1 Corinthians 12:12-30; Ephesians 4:4-6, 15-16; Colossians 1:18**

The people of God

The Old Testament describes how God called out an identifiable company, the Jews, not for favouritism but to be with him, to make known his grace to all and to be examples of faith and obedience.

The New Testament recognises that the Church is called to a like faith and obedience to Christ. As a pilgrim people, the Church proclaims the universal message of the grace of God and invites people everywhere to become fellow-pilgrims with those throughout the ages who have responded to God in faith.

■ **Exodus 19:5-6; Deuteronomy 27:9; Acts 5:29; 2 Corinthians 6:16; Titus 2:11-14; Hebrews 12:1-11; 13:14; 1 Peter 2:9-10; Revelation 21:3**

The community of reconciliation

The Church demonstrates that community has been restored through Christ. As the Fall brought division and deception into human relationships, so the restoration, if it was to be complete, had to bring healing, honesty and love into those relationships. The Church is the fellowship in which we learn to risk being vulnerable to one another because on the cross Christ conquered sin by making himself vulnerable for our sakes. The Church is called to demonstrate to the world that God has accomplished reconciliation through the Cross.

It must be admitted that there are many examples of Christian congregations failing to embody the reality of reconciliation both between believers and towards those outside the Christian community. In consequence, some have withdrawn from active participation in congregational life. However, total withdrawal from fellowship is a loss of Christian freedom and is a denial of one of the most significant benefits of the atonement.

But the body of Christ has not been, and is not, in bondage to its failures. Throughout the Church's history, where fellowship has been risked within the security Christ gives, spiritual transformation in human relationships has resulted. If we ask how such transformation has come about, the answer is, through the work of the Holy Spirit who creates, empowers and renews the Church. (*See chapter 5.*)

■ **Luke 14:15-24; John 15:1-11; 1 Corinthians 11:17-34; Galatians 6:2; Ephesians 2:11-22; 4:25-32; Colossians 1:1-22**

The continuing community

As an integral part of its mission to continue the ministry of Christ, the Church passes on the gospel from one generation to another. While subject to the authority of Scripture the Christian community, led by the Spirit, provides a consensus of interpretation that ensures the preservation of the gospel message.

The Church is one, though diverse in its expressions. Differing over certain matters, Christians are united in proclaiming Christ as the only Lord and Saviour, and the Church preserves a tradition of worship and devotion that originated with the first Christians and their response to the risen Lord.

Again and again in the New Testament we are reminded of the unity we already enjoy in Christ while, at the same time, we are warned against division and are exhorted to seek the greater completeness of that unity. All Christians are called constantly to pursue and express the unity God gives to his people.

The unity of the Church depends upon incorporation in Christ, not necessarily on organic union.

The challenge to unity reminds us that we live in a 'now but not yet' situation.

■ **Psalm 145:4-5; Matthew 18:20; John 17:20-26; Galatians 3:6-9**

The gathered community

The Church is created by the Holy Spirit for fellowship.

Together we are God's household, his family, as we abide in Christ and he in us. This intimate community is the work of the

Holy Spirit. It is he who enables us to gather in fellowship as one, sharing life together, growing up into Christ our head, discovering in him freedom from prejudice and sin.

The importance of such fellowship can hardly be overestimated. Within this community we experience healing, help and happiness. As holiness is relational, holiness of life is to be realised in community. As Christians we make our spiritual journey as part of a company. The New Testament speaks of 'saints' only in the plural. John Wesley taught that holiness is social: it is nurtured in the fellowship of Christians and then dispersed throughout society. (*See chapter 9.*)

■ **Luke 24:13-32; John 13:34-35; Acts 2:42-47; 4:32-35; Romans 12:15; 1 John 1; 4:7-12**

The Church is created by the Holy Spirit for healing.

Within Christ's healing community, the Holy Spirit enables us to care for each other, to respond to one another's hurts and to experience healing. Through the congregation the Spirit supports us in times of trial or loss; our personhood is affirmed and our worth enhanced. As we are being made holy and are helped and healed, we discover that the Church is a community of deep joy which no-one can take from us.

■ **James 5:13-20**

The Church is created by the Holy Spirit for nurture.

Within the Christian fellowship the Holy Spirit enables us to build each other up in the faith, to instruct, to bear each other's burdens, to encourage, forgive, celebrate, share, comfort and challenge one another.

Such strong support helps us to grow in Christlikeness and holiness and to cultivate the fruit of the Spirit. Described in Galatians 5:22-23 as love, joy, peace, patience, kindness, goodness, faithfulness, gentleness and self-control, the fruit of the Spirit is the manifestation of the nature of Christ in each of us through the sanctifying Spirit. It is the fruit that all Christians are called and empowered to bear and that marks us as true disciples of Jesus Christ.

We are also nurtured by the worship of the congregation. In worship, God edifies his people, enabling them to respond to the Holy Spirit for themselves and to reach out in faith to others. Prayer, preaching, music and artistic expression all combine to glorify God and nurture his people.

■ **Galatians 5:16-26; 6:1-6; Colossians 3:12-17; Philemon 7**

The Church is created by the Holy Spirit to equip for ministry and mission.

In the congregation we discover and deploy our individual gifts for ministry and mission. Each member of the body of Christ receives gifts for ministry and is called by God to develop and deploy them for the benefit of all. Gifts are given both to build up the Church and to make possible its mission in the world. The community of faith recognises our gifts and commissions our service. As we then deploy our gifts in ministry and mission, God is glorified. (*See appendix 8.*)

■ **Acts 6:1-6; 13:1-3; Romans 12:3-21; 1 Corinthians 7:7; 12:4-11; Ephesians 4:11-16; 1 Peter 4:7-11**

The sacramental community

Jesus Christ is the centre of the Church which lives to be a sign of God's grace in the world. As the sacramental community, the Church feeds upon him who is the one and only, true and original Sacrament. Christ is the source of grace from whom all other sacraments derive and to whom they bear witness. He is what is signified in the sign of the sacraments.

As the body of Christ the Church is his visible presence in the world. It is God's sign (sacrament) of the life together to which Christ calls the world, the visible expression of atoning grace. Rooted in the risen life of Christ, the one and only true, and original Sacrament, the Church daily discovers, celebrates – and is transformed by – his grace. It gathers around Jesus Christ, lives by faith in him and is blessed to be his sacramental community. The key features of this life are: genuine inclusiveness, radical obedience to God, simplicity of life, commitment to God's future in Christ and the celebration of God's gracious presence and work.

■ **Mark 6:8-9; John 6:52-63; 2 Corinthians 10:1-6; 2 Timothy 2:4; Hebrews 12:1-3; 25-29**

Celebration

It is true that the life we live is more important than the rituals we observe. The Old Testament prophets continually warned of the danger of placing undue value on religious ceremony to the exclusion of the values of compassionate action and ethical living and justice for the disadvantaged. Yet Jesus himself also recognised and honoured the importance of ritual and celebration in the life of the community of faith. He did not forbid their observance; he participated in them and often transformed them by pointing to himself as their focus and power.

Celebrations are needed in the life of any community, and celebrations of new life in Christ are needed in the life of the Church. Such celebrations are poignant ways for the Church to remind itself of that which God has done in Christ, that which is central to its faith and which transforms our lives. Celebrations and rituals can be vehicles through which the Holy Spirit brings renewal and hope to the fellowship of believers.

106

Celebrations of life in Christ point to and evoke deeper meanings and larger purposes. When they are practised in search of such meanings and purposes, and when they seek to merge the saving work of God with the broken life of humankind, they become occasions for the Spirit's transforming work. They become sacramental.

■ **Amos 5:21-24; Matthew 5:23; 8:1-4; Luke 2:21-24; 4:16; 17:11-14; 22:7-8; John 7:37-39; 13:1-20; Romans 2:28-29**

Sacraments

The majority of Christians find value in the ritual celebrations of baptism and communion. Since 1883, these have not been part of Salvationist practice. As God meets us in Jesus, we can receive his grace without prescribed rituals and experience real communion with him by the exercise of faith.

Through the simplicity and directness of our worship as well as our moments of community celebration, we are brought into the presence of Christ and invited to receive and grow in him. (*See appendix 9.*)

■ **Luke 22:14-23; John 6:52-63; Acts 2:41; Galatians 5:1-6; Ephesians 4:4-6; Colossians 2:9-12**

The scattered community

The Church gathers that it may be sent out in mission.

The Church is not a self-absorbed society brought together for security and socialising. It is a fellowship that releases its members for pilgrimage and mission. The Holy Spirit creates the Church not only for our benefit, but also to make our witness and mission possible.

■ **Matthew 9:35-10:16; 28:16-20; Mark 16:15; Luke 9:57-62; John 15:12-17**

The Holy Spirit empowers the whole Church for witness.

Our Christian pilgrimage demands an enduring commitment to a life of discipline and a tentative relationship to distracting world values. The Church is the community where Kingdom values are taught and lived, thereby encouraging us to sustain a radical lifestyle in keeping with our calling.

We are all called to live holy lives in the world and to see ourselves as set apart to be ministers or servants of the gospel. All Christians have direct access to God through the priesthood of Christ. All are called to exercise the challenging ministry of intercession on behalf of one another and for the world. In Christ, all Christians share in the priestly ministry. All vocations are important opportunities for expressing discipleship. In that sense there is no separated ministry.

Within that common calling, some are called by Christ to be full-time office-holders within the Church. Their calling is affirmed by the gift of the Holy Spirit, the recognition of the Christian community and their commissioning – ordination – for service. Their function is to focus the mission and ministry of the whole Church so that its members are held faithful to their calling.

They serve their fellow ministers as visionaries who point the way to mission, as pastors who minister to the priests when they are hurt or overcome, as enablers who equip others for mission, as spiritual leaders.

■ Acts 13:1-3; Ephesians 4:1-24; 1 Peter 2:4-10

The Holy Spirit empowers the Church for mission.

In affirming and sanctioning our callings, the Church sends us out to share in the mission of God who sent Jesus to reconcile the world to himself.

As members of Christ's Church we carry out God's mission in Christ's name in various ways including:

108

- by our presence in the world,

- by our public proclamation of the gospel,

- by personal evangelism,

- by pointing to evidence of the Holy Spirit's power to transform lives,

- by identifying with and offering compassionate service to the poor and disadvantaged,

- and by working with the oppressed for justice and liberty.

All of these ministries seek life-transformation. When any of them is ignored or neglected the mission of the Church suffers. As members of Christ's Church we are all engaged in mission to the whole person and the whole world through the power of the Holy Spirit.

■ **Matthew 5:13-16; 25:31-46; Mark 10:42-45; Luke 4:16-21; 10:25-37; Acts 8: 26-40; 2 Timothy 4:1-5**

A community renewed for the future

The Church lives by hope. It is caught up in the movement from Pentecost to the Parousia, from the beginning of the Church to the return of Christ and the fulfilment of his promises. The Holy Spirit frees God's resurrection people from the grip of past failures and renews them for God's future in Christ. The Bible looks to the future. In the Old Testament the restoration of Israel was promised. The New Testament sees this restoration on a universal scale: all things brought together under Christ.

In the Church, both militant on earth and triumphant in Heaven, God's future is not only hoped for, but also lived out. As such it is a sign of the coming Kingdom. The Church lives with its mind set on those things which are 'above'. It invests its talents and gifts to express that future and actually to live by its reality. The Church lives expectantly in the light of the dawn of Christ's future. Its mission is to open that future to the world.

■ **Jeremiah 31:1-14; Matthew 8:11; Mark 1:14-15; Romans 8:18-39; Ephesians 1:9-10; 1 Peter 1:3-9; 4:12-13; 5:10-11; Revelation 11:15; 21:1-4**

A summary

We believe in the Church, the body of Christ, justified and sanctified by grace, called to continue the mission and ministry of Christ.

Appendix 8

The use and abuse of spiritual gifts

Spiritual gifts are given by the Holy Spirit to unite the Christian fellowship in its life together and in its mission. As such, they are to be recognised as evidence of God's loving generosity to his people and of his desire that they be fully equipped to share in his mission.

In the New Testament there are a number of passages where specific spiritual gifts are identified. While these texts are not exhaustive, they speak of the many differing ministries that the Spirit has given to sustain the life of the Church. There are gifts that enable Christians to proclaim the gospel message, such as preaching, teaching and prophecy. Others are given so that Christians may serve people in Christ's name, for example, gifts of service, healing, generosity and hospitality. Some are gifts of leadership. Some are gifts which enhance and encourage devotion to God, such as gifts of prayer, faith and speaking in tongues. Whatever our gifts, they are to be used to serve one another and to glorify God.

It follows that the use of spiritual gifts to promote competition or to further individualism is misuse. We must beware, then, of the elevation of certain gifts as proof of spiritual superiority and the consequent undervaluing of other gifts.

Speaking in tongues is the clearest example of a gift that is overvalued in some Christian fellowships and undervalued in others. This gift is overvalued when it is regarded as the definitive evidence of the baptism in the Spirit and so becomes a measure of spiritual accomplishment. It is undervalued when it fails to be acknowledged as a true gift of God's Holy Spirit.

The Salvation Army recognises all spiritual gifts, including speaking in tongues. However, in the light of the susceptibility of the gift of tongues to abuse in public worship, the Army emphasises those gifts that encourage the clear proclamation of the gospel and draw into the circle of worship everyone who is present.

The New Testament shows that spiritual gifts are exercised in different ways in different congregations, often because of different circumstances and needs. It also emphasises the special value of those gifts that enable the Church clearly to present Jesus Christ as Lord and Saviour.

■ **See especially Romans 12:3-13; 1 Corinthians 12-14; Ephesians 4:7-13; 1 Peter 4:7-11.**

Appendix 9

The sacraments

A sacrament has been described as an outward and visible sign of inward and spiritual grace. It is a sign of grace that can be seen, smelled, heard, touched, tasted. It draws on the most common human experiences to express the most uncommon divine gifts. It takes what we take for granted and uses it to overwhelm us with the surprising grace of God.

A sacrament is an event in which the truths of our faith move into something that is quite beyond theological formulation and our attempts at comprehension. It brings the Incarnation to our doorstep, invites us to swing open the door of our intellectual caution and calls us to allow God's incomprehensible grace to enter – and transform – our ordinary lives. Sacraments deal with the extraordinary in the ordinary – extraordinary things like God's saving sacrifice, his inclusive fellowship, his call to discipleship, his forgiving family – ordinary things like a meal shared with those we care about, or a meal for strangers, water for washing, a flag to stand under, a joining of hands.

Christ, the one, true, original Sacrament, invites us to the ordinary, the common stuff of human existence, invites us to where he entered the scene in a stable, to where he subjected himself to an unsophisticated baptismal initiation rite, to where he sat at a humble table with family and friends, sinners and outcasts, to where a lively party was going on, to where he presided at a simple banquet using pieces of bread and a cup of wine to celebrate his coming death, the most significant event in the history of the human race. He invites us to the sacrament of his life, death and resurrection, the sacrament of the ordinary in the extraordinary.

As his sacramental people, we find him living and at work in our own life-experiences. We celebrate the presence, the gift, the healing, the reconciliation, the joy in our own story by connecting it with the story of Jesus.

We are a sacramental community because our life, our work, and our celebrations centre on Christ, the one true Sacrament. Our life together is sacramental because we live by faith in him and our everyday lives keep stumbling onto unexpected grace, his undeserved gift, again and again.

Early in our history, The Salvation Army chose not to observe specific sacraments as prescribed rituals. However, we do identify with the historic Church through its confession of one faith, one Lord, one baptism of the Holy Spirit, one salvation, and one Church universal. We confess one sacramental meal, not administered ritually, but presided over by Christ himself at any table where he is received and honoured.

We observe the sacraments, not by limiting them to two or three or seven, but by inviting Christ to suppers, love feasts, birth celebrations, parties, dedications, sick beds, weddings, anniversaries, commissionings, ordinations, retirements – and a host of other significant events – and, where he is truly received, watching him give a grace beyond our understanding. We can see, smell, hear, touch, and taste it. We joyfully affirm that in our presence is the one, true, original Sacrament. And we know that what we have experienced is reality.

CHAPTER ELEVEN

Kingdom of the risen Lord

The doctrine of Last Things

Related Doctrine

We believe in the immortality of the soul; in the resurrection of the body; in the general judgment at the end of the world; in the eternal happiness of the righteous; and in the endless punishment of the wicked.

The Christian hope in life after death depends upon belief in the resurrection of Jesus Christ. Belief in the resurrection asserts that death does not have the last word over human destiny: God does. Jesus conquered death, and so death does not finally separate us from God. He was raised from death to a new order of life, an eternal life given by God. The Christian hope is that as God raised Jesus Christ from death, so God will raise us from death to an eternal life with him.

For the Christian, belief in the resurrection is radical trust in the one, eternal God. The God of the beginning is also the God of the end. At the beginning there was God, who called the world into being out of nothing and created us in his own image. At the end there is God, not nothing; a God who calls us into new resurrection life with him. God, our creator and perfecter, completely fulfils his purpose for us.

As Jesus did not die into nothing, neither do we. We die into the life of God.

The triumph of the Kingdom of God

The completion of God's purposes for the whole universe can be illustrated in the biblical language of the Kingdom of God. This language is a way of describing the rule of God in human affairs, demonstrated when lives are transformed by Christ. The Bible looks forward to that transformation being made complete and visible in a new world order under God. This hope is clothed in vivid pictures which attempt to describe the ultimately indescribable, the entire cosmos in mutual harmony and at peace with its creator. There are descriptions of a new creation where all live in love, share an abundance of good things and know great joy. Images of banquets and wedding feasts, of water that never runs dry, of life-giving trees and an ever-welcoming eternal city express hope in concrete terms. They remind us that God plans for us a whole, fully personal eternal life together.

■ Isaiah 11:6-9; 65:17-25; Revelation 21:1-7; 22:1-5

Jesus came preaching the coming of God's Kingdom and in his ministry of teaching, preaching and healing revealed a foretaste of the coming joy. In Christ's resurrection from the dead and the outpouring of the Spirit, the life of the Kingdom of God was released into the world. All who accept Christ through faith can live in its reality and look forward to its completion at the end of time, when Christ returns. (*See appendix 10.*)

■ Luke 4:18-19; 7:22; 11:14-20; Acts 2:32-36; 1 Peter 1:3-5

Eternal life

The life beyond death which beckons the Christian is eternal life. This is a quality of life in the presence of God, not simply everlasting time. It begins now as we follow Christ. It is the life everlasting of which the Bible speaks, life with no end and love with no end. It is abundant life beyond our imagination. All we can say is that God will be all in all.

Eternal life focuses on unending adoration and enjoyment of God. We find our destiny and experience that for which we were created: to see God, to love him and to enjoy him for ever.

■ **Mark 10:17-22; John 3:16; 10:27-30; 11:25; 17:1-3; 1 Corinthians 2:9; 1 John 3:2**

Death and resurrection

To have a hope for Heaven is not to disguise the reality of death. Death is part of our human condition as biological beings. Death is God-given, a limitation on fallen human existence. But the reality of death should not deprive us of hope in the reality of death's defeat. Death does not separate us from God. Jesus has conquered death.

We will still die physically, yet because of Jesus Christ we need not be dead to God. When Paul writes about death being the 'wages of sin', he may be understood as referring to the spiritual death that threatens those who reject God.

■ **Psalm 116:15; Romans 6:23; 8:38-39; 1 Corinthians 15:20-26; Philippians 1:21-23**

The immortality of the soul

Christians have often expressed belief in life after death in the phrase, 'the immortality of the soul'. This phrase needs to be clearly understood. It is usually employed by Christians to mean that death is not the end, and this usual understanding is certainly essential to the gospel. It is important to recognise, however, that apart from God's action there is no part of us that naturally survives beyond death.

Our eternal existence is totally dependent on God. That is true for the righteous and the unrighteous. What the *Christian* doctrine of immortality says is that we are whole persons, originally brought to life by God, and because of God's action there is no loss of integrated, embodied personality in the life beyond present existence. God brings us all into eternity to participate in the general resurrection and submit to the final judgement of Christ.

■ Genesis 2:7; Mark 12:26-27; Romans 2:7; 1 Corinthians 15:50-54; 1 Timothy 6:13-16

The resurrection of the body

The phrase, 'the resurrection of the body' is the biblical way to express Christian belief in life after death. In the Bible the word 'body' means the whole person. The phrase safeguards the integrity of the human person. We do not look forward to becoming mere disembodied spirits, but whole persons, fully alive with Christ in God.

We all die, but death is not the end for either the believer or the non-believer. For all will be raised to judgement. Our life beyond the grave is entirely dependent upon the mercy and judgement of God, who has planned for those who trust in Jesus a re-creation into a new humanity, perfectly fulfilling his will.

Our resurrection depends upon the resurrection of Christ and follows a similar pattern. Jesus died a real death on the cross. His resurrection was a re-creation, not a resuscitation. He was not raised, like Lazarus, only to die again. He had a resurrection body different from his human body, yet recognisable. Our resurrection, too, through Christ, will be a total re-creation. Belief in a personal resurrection affirms our faith in God, creator and re-creator, who has made us, and will re-make us, out of love and for love.

■ **Job 19:25-27; Psalm 17:15; 49:14-15; 73:24; Isaiah 26:19; Daniel 12:2; John 5:25-29; 11:17-44; 1 Corinthians 15; Revelation 20:11-15**

Ultimate accountability

As Christians we believe that world history is not purposeless, but is moving towards an ultimate crisis, which biblical writers sometimes describe as 'the Day of the Lord'. In the Old Testament, the prophets used the term to look forward to the time when God's righteousness would be ultimately realised on earth, the day of triumph and transformation. The God of Israel would be revealed to all nations, for blessing and for judgement. The revelation of Jesus Christ changed the shape of this hope, though not its content, so that we now look forward to the time when Christ will be exalted and universally acknowledged as Lord.

■ **Isaiah 2:12-17; Joel 2:30-32; Amos 5:18-24; Philippians 2:9-11**

Judgement

It is in this context that we can speak of judgement. Judgement is the fulfilment of God's promises. It is the fullest affirmation of God's righteousness, of the liberating message of the New Testament, of the trusting faith of those who believe in a loving God. Judgement manifests the triumph of good over evil, the righting of wrongs, the validation of the truth, the victory of love over fear, the new Heaven and the new earth.

Judgement is also the fullest affirmation of universal accountability. All are accountable to God, during life and beyond death. This is the clear message of the New Testament. We have personal responsibility for our lives, for the choices we make, for our attitude and actions towards our fellows, for the stewardship of what we have received, for our ultimate destiny. This accountability is essential to our dignity as bearers of the divine image: God takes us seriously.

God alone is the judge. Because our judge is also our saviour, we can face judgement with confidence. His judgement will validate our faith-response. We can rest with assurance in the mercy of God, as well as in his absolute justice. We cannot dictate to God who will be saved and who not. But we can trust to the judgement of God the lives of all those whose life and experience, personal creed and spiritual opportunities are different from our own because he is the loving creator of all. (*See also 'The wrath of God', chapter 6.*)

■ **Psalm 9; Matthew 25:31-46; John 14:1-7; Romans 2:12-16; 11:32-36; 1 Corinthians 3:13-15; 1 John 4:17**

Hell and Heaven

To believe in judgement is to accept the reality of Hell and Heaven. Biblical pictures of Hell are terrifying and vivid and remind us that to choose to reject the grace of God must issue in a separation from him that reaches into eternity. Ultimately, our God-given freedom includes the freedom to make choices with eternal consequences. As Hell refers to the anguish of those who face eternity without God, so Heaven describes the bliss of those who enjoy the full experience of his presence. Biblical references to Heaven and Hell are only faint glimpses of the greater realities, of the final abode of the saved and the lost.

■ **Matthew 13:24-30; 25:1-13, 31-46; Mark 9:42-48; 2 Thessalonians 1:6-10; 2 Peter 3:8-13**

A hope to be shared

Christian life is marked by a hope that reaches beyond this life to life with God in his eternity. It is a life of joy in the presence of Christ, anticipating the life to come. It is a life of trust, full of confidence in the ultimate purposes of God in Christ.

For us, the future hope is already part of the present, as the Holy Spirit brings to us the living Christ, who makes his Kingdom a present reality. As we live out this future today, we invite others to share in our hope.

A summary

We believe in Christ's return in glory, the completion of God's Kingdom, the resurrection of the body, the final accountability of all persons to God, Heaven and Hell, the endless despair of those who reject salvation and the eternal happiness of those who are righteous through faith.

Appendix 10

Interpretations of the return of Christ

The Salvation Army has avoided speculation about details of the return of Christ. Salvationists prefer to emphasise the Christian responsibility to live in a state of expectation and hope. We should be constantly open to the presence and judgement of God in Christ, and fully involved in the mission of God for the salvation of the world.

The following definitions may be of help to those in dialogue with fellow Christians on these matters.

The *millennium* refers to the thousand-year reign of Christ on earth which is mentioned in Revelation 20: 2-7.

Some Christians interpret the millennium symbolically to mean, not a period of time as such, but Christ's reign on earth through his people. This is usually known as *a-millennialism.*

Others teach a more literal interpretation. *Post-millennialists* teach that there will be a period of the Kingdom of God on earth, or a thousand years of 'power for the gospel' followed by the return of Christ. In contrast, *pre-millennialists* teach that Christ will return to earth to reign for a thousand years before Satan's final overthrow.

Dispensationalists take the pre-millennial view further. They see the millennium as a further dispensation, or period in God's dealings with humanity. In their understanding, the coming of Christ will be preceded by the 'rapture' of the Church. The millennium itself will be the time of the literal fulfilment of the Old Testament promises to Israel.

So many differing interpretations suggest that the Bible leaves us with the mystery of God and his purposes for us, which are finally beyond speculation. Our best response is to be silent before the mystery, confident before the promise and trusting before a loving God revealed to us in Jesus Christ.

Appendix 11

The Classical Creeds

An introduction

The historic creeds have come to us from the earliest days of Christianity. They have sought to state briefly and comprehensively what Christians believe. Their purpose has been twofold. They are a confession of faith, a common testimony to the truth as received in Jesus Christ. They are also a defence of sound teaching, seeking in their words to exclude error and define truth.

Their beginnings lie in the definitions of Christian experience and faith contained in the New Testament. The earliest confessions of belief were short and simple; for example, 'Jesus is Lord' (1 Corinthians 12:3) or 'I believe that Jesus Christ is the Son of God' (Acts 8:37). They developed into more comprehensive statements recited as baptismal confessions of faith by converts when admitted to the fellowship of believers. They were the password into the community of the Christian Church. Later, in the fourth century, the great ecumenical councils of the Church met to refute heresy and more accurately define orthodox faith by the development of commonly agreed statements of belief.

The Apostles Creed is built on what scholars refer to as the Old Roman Creed from the early third century, and represents a lengthy development from the earlier simple trinitarian baptismal formula. While it is not apostolic in authorship, it is nevertheless apostolic in content. It describes the fundamental articles of the Christian faith. The Old Roman Creed was written in Latin but there was a more or less identical older Greek version. The Apostles Creed begins with 'I believe', which is different from some of the later creeds formulated by Church councils, which begin with 'we believe'.

The Nicene Creed was probably based on earlier creeds from Jerusalem and Antioch. Its purpose was to define the true faith as over against the teaching of certain heretics. It expresses the faith of the first Ecumenical Council in Nicea in 325, which was enlarged and approved by the Council of Constantinople in 381 and confirmed by the Council of Chalcedon in 451. It affirms the unity of God, insists that the Son is God in every respect, and upholds the divinity of the Holy Spirit.

The Creed of Nicea is the most ecumenical of the creeds as it is accepted both in the Eastern and Western churches. Even though it is an ecumenical creed, there is a difference in the statement about the Holy Spirit, which was the cause of a schism between the Eastern and Western churches in 1054. The Latin form of the creed states that the Holy Spirit 'proceeds from the Father and the Son', while the Eastern church keeps the original Greek version, 'proceeds from the Father'. This difference is still a difficulty. (See page 51.)

The Athanasian Creed was formulated in the mid-5th century in Spain or France by an unknown author from the Augustinian tradition. It was written as an instrument of teaching. Later it was used in the services as a credal hymn. It contains a clear and concise statement of the Trinity and the Incarnation of Christ. This creed is not as widespread in its use as the Apostles Creed and the Nicene Creed.

We can have confidence in the teaching of the creeds, which bring the basic truths of Christianity to us from the days of the New Testament. They flow like a majestic river from the springs of the proclamation of the Apostles and the life and teaching of the Lord Jesus Christ.

The Apostles Creed

I BELIEVE in God the Father almighty, Maker of heaven and earth:

And in Jesus Christ His only Son our Lord, who was conceived by the Holy Ghost, born of the Virgin Mary, suffered under Pontius Pilate, was crucified, dead and buried; He descended into hell; the third day He rose again from the dead. He ascended into heaven, and sitteth on the right hand of God the Father almighty; from thence He shall come to judge the quick and the dead.

I believe in the Holy Ghost, the holy catholic Church, the communion of saints, the forgiveness of sins, the resurrection of the body, and the life everlasting.

The Nicene Creed

I BELIEVE in one God the Father almighty, Maker of heaven and earth, and of all things visible and invisible.

And in one Lord Jesus Christ, the only-begotten Son of God, begotten of His Father before all worlds, God of God, Light of Light, very God of very God, begotten, not made, being of one substance with the Father, by whom all things were made:

Who for us men and for our salvation came down from heaven, and was incarnate by the Holy Ghost of the Virgin Mary, and was made man, and was crucified also for us under Pontius Pilate. He suffered and was buried, and the third day He rose again according to the Scriptures, and ascended into heaven, and sitteth on the right hand of the Father. And he shall come again with glory to judge both the quick and the dead; whose kingdom shall have no end.

And I believe in the Holy Ghost, Lord and Giver of life, who proceedeth from the Father and the Son, who with the Father and the Son together is worshipped and glorified, who spake by the prophets.

And I believe in one holy catholic and apostolic Church. I acknowledge one baptism for the remission of sins. And I look for the resurrection of the dead, and the life of the world to come.

The Athanasian Creed

WHOSOEVER wills to be in a state of salvation, before all things it is necessary that he hold the catholic [apostolic/universal] faith, which except everyone shall have kept whole and undefiled without doubt he shall perish eternally.

Now the catholic faith is that we worship One God in Trinity and Trinity in Unity; neither confounding the Persons nor dividing the substance. For there is one Person of the Father, another of the Son, and another of the Holy Spirit. But the Godhead of the Father, of the Son and of the Holy Spirit, is One, the Glory equal, the Majesty coeternal.

Such as the Father is, such is the Son, and such is the Holy Spirit, the Father uncreated, the Son uncreated, and the Holy Ghost uncreated; the Father infinite, the Son infinite, and the Holy Spirit infinite, the Father eternal, the Son eternal, and the Holy Spirit eternal. And yet not three eternals but one eternal, as also not three infinites, nor three uncreated, but one uncreated, and one infinite. So, likewise, the Father is almighty, the Son almighty, and the Holy Spirit almighty, and yet they are not three Almighties but one Almighty.

So the Father is God, the Son God, and the Holy Spirit God; and yet they are not three Gods but one God. So the Father is Lord, the Son Lord, and the Holy Spirit Lord; and yet not three Lords but one Lord. For like as we are compelled by the

Christian truth to acknowledge every Person by Himself to be God and Lord; so we are forbidden by the catholic religion to say, there be three Gods or three Lords.

The Father is made of none, neither created nor begotten. The Son is of the Father alone, not made nor created but begotten. The Holy Spirit is of the Father and the Son, not made nor created nor begotten but proceeding. So there is one Father not three Fathers, one Son not three Sons, and one Holy Spirit not three Holy Spirits. And in this Trinity there is nothing before or after, nothing greater or less, but the whole three Persons are coeternal together and co-equal.

So that in all things, as is aforesaid, the Trinity in Unity and the Unity in Trinity is to be worshipped. He therefore who wills to be in a state of salvation, let him thus think of the Trinity.

But it is necessary to eternal salvation that he also believe faithfully the Incarnation of our Lord Jesus Christ. For the right faith therefore is that we believe and confess that our Lord Jesus Christ, the Son of God, is God and Man.

He is God of the substance of the Father begotten before the worlds, and He is man of the substance of His mother born in the world; perfect God, perfect man subsisting of a reasoning soul and human flesh; equal to the Father as touching His Godhead, and inferior to the Father as touching His Manhood.

Who although He be God and Man yet He is not two but one Christ; one however not by conversion of the Godhead in the flesh, but by taking of the Manhood in God; one altogether not by confusion of substance but by unity of Person. For as the reasoning soul and flesh is one man, so God and Man is one Christ.

Who suffered for our salvation, descended into hell, rose again from the dead, ascended into heaven, sits on the right hand of the Father, from whence He shall come to judge the living and the dead. At whose coming all men shall rise again with their bodies and shall give account of their own works. And they that have done good shall go into life eternal, and they who indeed have done evil into eternal fire.

This is the catholic faith, which except a man shall have believed faithfully and firmly, he cannot be in a state of salvation.

Glory be to the Father, and to the Son, and to the Holy Spirit; as it was in the beginning, is now, and ever shall be: world without end. Amen.

Appendix 12

Sources of the Eleven Articles of Faith

Over the centuries since the classical creeds were written, further credal statements have come into being, associated with particular church groupings. Used in conjunction with the three creeds, they identify the distinctive doctrinal emphases of the group concerned. Examples of these are the Westminster Confession, which is still regarded as definitive in Presbyterian Churches, and the Augustana, which from the time of the Reformation has marked the distinctive tenets of Lutheranism.

Our Salvation Army Articles of Faith fulfil a similar function. While their origin is nowhere stated, their roots are clearly in the Wesleyan tradition. The articles bear a striking similarity in words and content to Methodist New Connexion doctrines, which can be traced back to at least 1838. William Booth was an ordained minister of the New Connexion, whose founders claimed their doctrines to be 'those of Methodism, as taught by Mr Wesley'. With the Movement's birth in 1865, William Booth adopted seven articles of belief. Three more were added in 1870 and the last, now number ten, in 1876. Each additional point can be traced back to the New Connexion document. With only slight editorial modifications, chiefly of punctuation, these Articles are placed as Schedule 1 of The Salvation Army Act, 1980.

Our doctrinal statement, then, derives from the teaching of John Wesley and the evangelical awakening of the eighteenth and nineteenth centuries. While there was significant correspondence between evangelicals in the mid-nineteenth century, indicated especially in the eight-point statement of the Evangelical Alliance of 1846, the distinctives of Salvation Army doctrine came from Methodism. Our strong emphasis on regeneration and sanctification, our conviction that the gospel is for the whosoever and our concern for humanity's free will all find their roots there.

The Doctrines of the Methodist New Connexion (1838) follow in this appendix.

The Doctrines of the Methodist New Connexion (1838)

1. **We believe** that there is one God, who is infinitely perfect, The Creator, Preserver and Governor of all things.

2. **We believe** that the Scriptures of the Old and New Testaments are given by Divine Inspiration and form a complete rule of faith and practice.

3. **We believe** that three persons exist in the Godhead: the Father, the Son, and the Holy Ghost, undivided in essence, and co-equal in power and glory.

4. **We believe** that in the person of Jesus Christ the divine and human natures are united, so that he is truly and properly God, and truly and properly man.

5. **We believe** that man was created in righteousness and true holiness, but that by his disobedience, Adam lost the purity and happiness of his nature; and, in consequence, all his posterity are involved in depravity and guilt.

6. **We believe** that Jesus Christ has become the propitiation for the sins of the whole world, that he rose from the dead, and that he ever liveth to make intercession for us.

7. **We believe** that repentance toward God, and faith in our Lord Jesus Christ, are necessary to salvation.

8. **We believe** that justification is by grace, through faith, and that he that believeth hath the witness in himself: and that it is our privilege to be fully sanctified in the name of the Lord Jesus Christ, and by the spirit of our God.

9. **We believe** that man's salvation is of God, and that his damnation is of himself. We believe, also, that in the Gospel plan of redemption, men are treated as rational, accountable creatures; that 'it is God that worketh in us to will and to do of his own good pleasure;' and that we are to 'work out our own salvation, with fear and trembling'.

10. **We believe** that it is possible for man to fall finally from grace.

11. **We believe** the soul to be immortal, and that after death it immediately enters upon a state of happiness or misery.

12. **We believe** in the resurrection of the body – in the general judgement at the last day – in the eternal happiness of the righteous – and in the endless punishment of the wicked.

Appendix 13

The Lausanne Covenant

An introduction

The Lausanne Covenant was drafted by the Congress on World Evangelisation held in 1974 in Lausanne, Switzerland. On that occasion, 2,700 participants from 150 nations voiced their praise to God for his salvation and rejoiced in the evangelical fellowship they discovered in obedience to the Great Commission of their Lord: 'Therefore go and make disciples of all nations, baptising them in the name of the Father and of the Son and of the Holy Spirit, and teaching them to obey everything I have commanded you' (Matthew 28:19-20).

The adoption of the Lausanne Covenant marked a theological consensus amongst evangelicals on the basis and nature of evangelisation. Because the evangelical constituency which gathered on that occasion was so diverse in terms of nationality, culture, denominationalism, theological beliefs and programme priorities, arriving at such a consensus was considered a watershed occasion for the twentieth-century evangelical community.

The Lausanne Covenant provided a foundation for subsequent meetings of evangelicals. In 1982, a further major consultation of 50 evangelical leaders from six continents was convened in Grand Rapids, Michigan to clarify the relationship between evangelism and social responsibility. That discussion focussed on article five of the Lausanne Covenant on 'Christian Social Responsibility'.

Another aspect of the Lausanne Covenant was developed at Lausanne II when in l989 over 3,000 delegates from 170 countries met in Manila in the Philippines with the theme, 'Calling the Whole Church to take the Whole Gospel to the Whole World'. The Manila Manifesto was issued from this consultation and The Salvation Army endorsed that statement as part of its Vision 2000 direction for the decade of the 90's.

It may be too early to consider the Lausanne Covenant as a 'creed' in the classical sense of that term. It is included in this appendix of *Salvation Story* as having relevance to the substance of this handbook. It has the potential of providing the basis for a credal statement arising from evangelicals as they seek unitedly to meet the increasingly complex challenge of each age to communicate the *Salvation Story* and to win the world for Christ.

The Covenant

Let the earth hear his voice

Introduction

We, members of the Church of Jesus Christ, from more than 150 nations, participants in the International Congress on World Evangelisation at Lausanne, praise God for his great salvation and rejoice in the fellowship he has given us with himself and with each other. We are deeply stirred by what God is doing in our day, moved to penitence by our failures and challenged by the unfinished task of evangelisation. We believe the gospel is God's Good News for the whole world, and we are determined by his grace to obey Christ's commission to proclaim it to every person and to make disciples of every nation. We desire, therefore, to affirm our faith and our resolve, and to make public our covenant.

1. The Purpose of God

We affirm our belief in the one eternal God, Creator and Lord of the world, Father, Son, and Holy Spirit, who governs all things according to the purpose of his will. He has been calling out from the world a people for himself, and sending his people back into the world to be his servants and his witnesses, for the extension of his kingdom, the building up of Christ's body, and the glory of his name. We confess with shame that we have often denied our calling and failed in our mission, by becoming conformed to the world or by withdrawing from it. Yet, we rejoice that even when borne by earthen vessels the gospel is still a precious treasure. To the task of making that treasure known in the power of the Holy Spirit we desire to dedicate ourselves anew.

2. The Authority and Power of the Bible

We affirm the divine inspiration, truthfulness and authority of both Old and New Testament Scriptures in their entirety as the only written Word of God, without error in all that it affirms, and the only infallible rule of faith and practice. We also affirm the power of God's Word to accomplish his purpose of salvation. The message of the Bible is addressed to all men and women. For God's revelation in Christ and in Scripture is unchangeable. Through it the Holy Spirit still speaks today. He illumines the minds of God's people in every culture to perceive its truth freshly through their own eyes and thus discloses to the whole church ever more of the many coloured wisdom of God.

3. The Uniqueness and Universality of Christ

We affirm that there is only one Saviour and only one gospel, although there is a wide diversity of evangelistic approaches. We recognise that everyone has some knowledge of God through his general revelation in nature. But we deny that this can save, for people suppress the truth by their unrighteousness. We also reject as derogatory to Christ and the gospel every kind of syncretism and dialogue which implies that Christ speaks equally through all religions and ideologies. Jesus Christ, being himself the only God-man, who gave himself as the only ransom for sinners, is the only mediator between God and people. There is no other name by which we must be saved. All men and women are perishing because of sin, but God loves everyone, not wishing that any should perish but that all should repent. Yet those who reject Christ repudiate the joy of salvation and condemn themselves to eternal separation from God. To proclaim Jesus as 'the Saviour of the world' is not to affirm that all people are either automatically or ultimately saved, still less to affirm that all religions offer salvation in Christ. Rather it is to proclaim God's love for a world of sinners and to invite everyone to respond to him as Saviour and Lord in the whole-hearted personal commitment of repentance and faith. Jesus Christ has been exalted above every other name; we long for the day when every knee shall bow to him and every tongue shall confess him Lord.

4. The Nature of Evangelism

To evangelise is to spread the Good News that Jesus Christ died for our sins and was raised from the dead according to the Scriptures, and that as the reigning Lord he now offers the forgiveness of sins and the liberating gift of the Spirit to all who repent and believe. Our Christian presence in the world is indispensable to evangelism, and so is that kind of dialogue whose purpose is to listen sensitively in order to understand. But evangelism itself is the proclamation of the historical, biblical Christ as Saviour and Lord, with a view to persuading people to come to him personally and so be reconciled to God. In issuing the gospel invitation we have no liberty to conceal the cost of discipleship. Jesus still calls all who would follow him to deny themselves, take up their cross, and identify themselves with his new community. The results of evangelism include obedience to Christ, incorporation into his church and responsible service in the world.

5. Christian Social Responsibility

We affirm that God is both the Creator and the Judge of all. We, therefore, should share his concern for justice and reconciliation throughout human society and for the liberation of men and women from every kind of oppression. Because men and women are made in the image of God, every person, regardless of race, religion, colour, culture, class, sex, or age, has intrinsic dignity because of which he or she should be respected and served, not exploited. Hereto we express penitence both for our neglect and for having sometimes regarded evangelism and social concern as mutually exclusive. Although reconciliation with other people is not reconciliation with God, nor is social action evangelism, nor is political liberation salvation, nevertheless we affirm that evangelism and socio-political involvement are both part of our Christian duty. For both are necessary expressions of our doctrines of God and man, our love for our neighbour and our obedience to Jesus Christ. The message of salvation implies also a message of judgment upon every form of alienation, oppression, and discrimination, and we should not be afraid to denounce evil and injustice wherever they exist. When people receive Christ they are born again into his kingdom and must seek not only to exhibit but also to spread its righteousness in the midst of an unrighteous world. The salvation we claim should be transforming us in the totality of our personal and social responsibilities. Faith without works is dead.

6. The Church and Evangelism

We affirm that Christ sends his redeemed people into the world as the Father sent him, and that this calls for a similar deep and costly penetration of the world. We need to break out of our ecclesiastical ghettos and permeate non-Christian society. In the church's mission of sacrificial service evangelism is primary. World evangelisation requires the whole church to take the whole gospel to the whole world. The church is at the very centre of God's cosmic purpose and is his appointed means of spreading the gospel. But a church which preaches the cross must itself be marked by the cross. It becomes a stumbling block to evangelism when it betrays the gospel or lacks a living faith in God, a genuine love for people, or scrupulous honesty in all things including promotion and finance. The church is the community of God's people rather than an institution, and must not be identified with any particular culture, social, or political system, or human ideology.

7. Co-operation in Evangelism

We affirm that the church's visible unity in truth is God's purpose. Evangelism also summons us to unity, because our oneness strengthens our witness, just as our disunity undermines our gospel of reconciliation. We recognize, however, that organisational unity may take many forms and does not necessarily forward evangelism. Yet, we who share the same biblical faith should be closely united in fellowship, work, and witness. We confess that our testimony has sometimes been marred by sinful individualism and needless duplication. We pledge ourselves to seek a deeper unity in truth, worship, holiness, and mission. We urge the development of regional and functional cooperation for furtherance of the church's mission, for strategic planning, for mutual encouragement, and for the sharing of resources and experience.

8. Churches in Evangelistic Partnership

We rejoice that a new missionary era has dawned. The dominant role of western missions is fast disappearing. God is raising up from the younger churches a great new resource for world evangelisation, and is, thus, demonstrating that the responsibility to evangelise belongs to the whole body of Christ. All churches should, therefore, be asking God and themselves what they should be doing both to reach their own area and to send missionaries to other parts of the world. A re-evaluation of our missionary responsibility and role should be continuous. Thus, a growing partnership of churches will develop and the universal character of Christ's church will be more clearly exhibited. We also thank God for agencies which labour in Bible translation, theological education, the mass media, Christian literature, evangelism, missions, church renewal and other specialist fields. They, too, should engage in constant self-examination to evaluate their effectiveness as part of the church's mission.

9. The Urgency of the Evangelistic Task

More than 2,700 million people, which is more than two-thirds of all humanity, have yet to be evangelised. We are ashamed that so many have been neglected; it is a standing rebuke to us and to the whole church. There is now, however, in many parts of the world an unprecedented receptivity to the Lord Jesus Christ. We are convinced that this is the time for churches and para-church agencies to pray earnestly for the salvation of the unreached and to launch new efforts to achieve world evangelisation. A reduction of foreign missionaries and money in an evangelised country may sometimes be necessary to facilitate the national church's growth in self-reliance and to release resources for unevangelised areas. Missionaries should flow ever more freely from and to all six continents in a spirit of humble service. The goal should be, by all available means and at the earliest possible time, that every person will have the opportunity to hear, understand, and receive the Good News. We cannot hope to attain this goal without sacrifice. All of us are shocked by the poverty of millions and disturbed by the injustices which cause it. Those of us who live in affluent circumstances accept our duty to develop a simple lifestyle in order to contribute more generously to both relief and evangelism.

10. Evangelism and Culture

The development of strategies for world evangelisation calls for imaginative pioneering methods. Under God, the result will be the rise of churches deeply rooted in Christ and closely related to their culture. Culture must always be tested and judged by Scripture. Because men and women are God's creatures, some of their culture is rich in beauty and goodness. Because they are fallen, all of it is tainted with sin and some of it is demonic. The gospel does not presuppose the superiority of any culture to another, but evaluates all cultures according to its own criteria of truth and righteousness, and insists on moral absolutes in every culture. Missions have all too frequently exported with the gospel an alien culture and churches have sometimes been in bondage to culture rather than to Scripture. Christ's evangelists must humbly seek to empty themselves of all but their personal authenticity in order to become the servants of others, and churches must seek to transform and enrich culture, all for the glory of God.

11. Education and Leadership

We confess that we have sometimes pursued church growth at the expense of church depth, and divorced evangelism from Christian nurture. We also acknowledge that some of our missions have been too slow to equip and encourage national leaders to assume their rightful responsibilities. Yet, we are committed to indigenous principles, and long that every church will have national leaders who manifest a Christian style of leadership in terms not of domination but of service. We recognise that there is a great need to improve theological education, especially for church leaders. In every nation and culture there should be an effective training programme for pastors, and laity in doctrine, discipleship, evangelism, nurture, and service. Such training programmes should not rely on any stereotyped methodology but should be developed by creative local initiatives according to biblical standards.

12. Spiritual Conflict

We believe that we are engaged in constant spiritual warfare with the principalities and powers of evil, who are seeking to overthrow the church and frustrate its task of world evangelisation. We know our need to equip ourselves with God's armour and to fight this battle with the spiritual weapons of truth and prayer. For we detect the activity of our enemy, not only in false ideologies outside the church, but also inside it in false gospels which twist Scripture and put people in the place of God. We need both watchfulness and discernment to safeguard the biblical gospel. We acknowledge that we ourselves are not immune to worldliness of thought and action, that is, to a surrender to secularism. For example, although careful studies of church growth, both numerical and spiritual, are right and valuable, we have sometimes neglected them. At other times, desirous to ensure a response to the gospel, we have compromised our message, manipulated our hearers through pressure techniques, and become unduly preoccupied with statistics or even dishonest in our use of them. All this is worldly. The church must be in the world; the world must not be in the church.

13. Freedom and Persecution

It is the God-appointed duty of every government to secure conditions of peace, justice, and liberty in which the church may obey God, serve the Lord Christ, and preach the gospel without interference. We, therefore, pray for the leaders of the nations and call upon them to guarantee freedom of thought and conscience, and freedom to practice and propagate religion in accordance with the will of God and as set forth in 'The Universal Declaration of Human Rights.' We also express our deep concern for all who have been unjustly imprisoned, and especially for those who are suffering for their testimony to the Lord Jesus. We promise to pray and work for their freedom. At the same time we refuse to be intimidated by their fate. God helping us, we, too, will seek to stand against injustice and to remain faithful to the gospel, whatever the cost. We do not forget the warnings of Jesus that persecution is inevitable.

14. The Power of the Holy Spirit

We believe in the power of the Holy Spirit. The Father sent his Spirit to bear witness to his Son; without his witness ours is futile. Conviction of sin, faith in Christ, new birth, and Christian growth are all his work. Further, the Holy Spirit is a missionary spirit; thus, evangelism should arise spontaneously from a Spirit-filled church. A church that is not a missionary church is contradicting itself and quenching the Spirit. Worldwide evangelisation will become a realistic possibility only when the Spirit renews the church in truth and wisdom, faith, holiness, love and power. We, therefore, call upon all Christians to pray for such a visitation of the sovereign Spirit of God that all his fruit may appear in all his people and that all his gifts may enrich the body of Christ. Only then will the whole church become a fit instrument in his hands, that the whole earth may hear his voice.

15. The Return of Christ

We believe that Jesus Christ will return personally and visibly, in power and glory, to consummate his salvation and his judgment. This promise of his coming is a further spur to our evangelism, for we remember his words that the gospel must first be preached to all nations. We believe that the interim period between Christ's ascension and return is to be filled with the mission of the people of God, who have no liberty to stop before the end. We also remember his warning that false Christs and false prophets will arise as precursors of the final Antichrist. We, therefore, reject as a proud, self-confident dream the notion that people can ever build a utopia on earth. Our Christian confidence is that God will perfect his kingdom, and we look forward with eager anticipation to that day, and to the new heaven and earth in which righteousness will dwell and

God will reign forever. Meanwhile, we rededicate ourselves to the service of Christ and of people in joyful submission to his authority over the whole of our lives.

Conclusion

Therefore, in the light of this our faith and our resolve, we enter into a solemn covenant with God and with each other, to pray, to plan, and to work together for the evangelization of the whole world. We call upon others to join us. May God help us by his grace and for his glory to be faithful to this our covenant! Amen, Allelujah!

(International Congress on World Evangelisation, Lausanne, Switzerland, July 1974, copyright Lausanne Committee for World Evangelisation, used by permission).

Glossary of doctrinal terms

abba: a common Aramaic word from the time of Jesus meaning 'father', expressing the closest possible father-child relationship

adoptionism: belief that Jesus was only human and chosen as Son of God during his lifetime (*see appendix 4*)

Apocrypha: 'hidden writings' – ancient writings whose place in Scripture is disputed (*appendix 1*)

apostolic: with the authority, from the time, or in the tradition of the apostles

Arianism: an early heresy that essentially denied the full divinity of Jesus Christ (*appendix 4*)

assurance: confidence in the reality of personal salvation, made possible by the work of the Holy Spirit

atonement: literally, 'at-one-ment', restoration of a right relationship with God

canon: (canonical) literally, 'a rod or measuring stick', the universally accepted list of books belonging within the Bible

catholic: from a Greek word meaning 'universal' and referring to the Church as a whole, not a particular denomination conversion: the act of turning to Christ, including both repentance and saving faith

covenant: a binding agreement between two parties; (covenantal) in Scripture, the agreement offered to humanity by God of loving faithfulness in return for complete devotion

creed: a corporate statement of belief, used to (credal) express commitment to the faith

deism: a belief that God exists, while denying that he actively reveals himself or intervenes in the world in any way (*appendix 3*)

demonic: pertaining to the devil or evil supernatural powers

depravity: the corrupted, perverted nature of (total) humanity under the power of original sin

docetism: a heresy which essentially denied the full humanity of Jesus Christ (*appendix 4*)

dualism: the belief that there are two co-equal (dualistic) eternal realities, one good and the other evil

Ebionitism: an early heresy that regarded Jesus as a purely human figure, though specially gifted by God (*appendix 4*)

faith: confident, obedient trust in the living God

grace: the persistent, loving favour of God towards undeserving humanity

heresy: belief which is contrary to Christian (heretical) doctrine

humanism: (humanist)	a belief that humanity in itself is capable of improving the world by moral development and education
immortality:	life untouched by decay and death, never ending, eternal life
inbred sin:	the corrupted, perverted nature of humanity under the power of original sin
Incarnation: (incarnate)	the act of becoming flesh, as God took on full humanity for our salvation and became a man in Jesus of Nazareth
inspiration:	literally 'in-breathing', the stimulation of the mind, spirit or creative abilities by the aid of the Holy Spirit
justification:	God's act of declaring people to be righteous before him, accepting them despite their past sins
millennialism:	beliefs connected with the end times, especially that the Kingdom of God will flourish for a thousand years on earth (*appendix 10*)
modalism:	a doctrine of God which denies that there are three distinct persons in the Godhead; each person is seen as one aspect, or mode, of God's existence (*appendix 3*)
monotheism:	the belief that there is only one God
mythology: (mythologies)	traditional narratives which express world views and truths, and explain moral codes and religious rituals
original sin:	the inclination to sin which arises from the Fall, and is basic to fallen human nature

orthodoxy: literally 'right teaching', belief consistent with Christian truth

pantheism: the belief that all living things are divine, and so the objects of worship (*appendix 3*)

parousia: the return of Christ in glory, often referred to as the Second Coming

Pentecost: the name for the Jewish Feast of Weeks, associated by Christians with the first, great outpouring of the Holy Spirit and the beginning of the Christian Church

pluralism: the existence of many ethnic and religious (pluralist) groups in society or the belief that all religious views are equally valid

polytheism: belief in and worship of more than one God (*appendix 3*)

predestination: a belief of some Christians that God has already determined who will be saved

prevenient grace: literally 'grace' which 'comes before', the action by which God prepares and helps the hearer to seek him and find salvation

regeneration: literally 're-birth', the renewal by the Holy Spirit which comes with the acceptance of God's grace

re-incarnation: the belief that all souls are immortal and live many succeeding lives on earth

repentance: change of direction; the action of turning away from sin and towards God

revelation: God's action in making himself known to the world

righteousness: (righteous)
being in a right relationship with God and people

sacrament: (sacramental)
an action or ceremony used in Christian worship which is an outward sign and has an inner meaning (*chapter 10, The sacramental community; appendix 9*)

sanctification:
the crisis and process by which the Christian's life and character become Christlike, through the work of the Holy Spirit

subordinationism:
a belief that God the Son and God the Holy Spirit are inferior to God the Father

syncretism:
an attempt to combine distinct and different religious teaching, a mixture of religious ideas from many sources

transcendence:
God's nature which extends beyond the limitations of his creation

Trinity: (triune, trinitarianism)
belief in one God who is at the same time Father, Son and Holy Spirit

tritheism:
belief that the Trinity is not one God but three

vicarious:
something borne or done on behalf of another, used especially of the sacrifice of Christ on the cross

wrath: (of God)
God's active opposition to evil in all its forms, the other side of his love

Glossary of English usage

accountability:	responsibility, to others or to God
allegiance:	loyalty to authorities or to God
awe:	reverential fear or wonder in the presence of God
beguile:	cheat, seduce, divert attention
community:	body of people with shared identity, goals and relationships
consensus:	agreement by reaching common ground
consummation:	completion; reaching the desired end; fulfilment
corporate:	having to do with a body of people rather than an individual
cosmos:	the universe as an ordered whole
deity:	divine status; divinity
destiny:	final goal or purpose of existence
dilemma:	having to choose between difficult alternatives
empower: (empowerment)	to give authority with support; to enable

essence:	basic nature or quality
faulty:	imperfect, untrue
foreshadow:	to give a prior sign with characteristics of what is to come
foretaste:	prospect; advance enjoyment
foundational:	basic
guarantee:	pledge; security; token of commitment
hallmark:	mark used by goldsmiths to confirm a standard
hierarchy:	organised, graded status
inaugurate:	begin, initiate
indifferent:	uninterested, uncaring
integral:	necessary to the whole; essential
investment:	something used or given to produce growth
jealous:	pained by unfaithfulness
luminous:	giving off light
lurking:	hidden; watching without being seen, usually with evil intent
malevolent: (malevolence)	desiring evil to others
manifestation:	revelation, clear evidence or proof
mar:	ruin or spoil
mysticism:	the practice of contemplating mysteries and/or seeking union with the divine

neo-paganism:	new versions of pagan beliefs
overwhelming:	overpowering
pervasive:	spread throughout
philosophy:	love of knowledge or truth
precursor:	forerunner; something that goes before
potency:	power; might; strength
radical:	springing from its root and returning to basic principles
ransom:	sum of money or value paid for release
reconciliation:	coming together following separation, the healing of broken relationships
remorse:	deep regret for wrong done
resuscitate:	revive, restore to life
simultaneous:	occurring or operating at the same time
spiritism:	communication with departed spirits
substitute:	someone who fills a place for another
tangible:	what can be touched or clearly grasped
thwart:	frustrate, prevent
traumatic:	involving deep emotional upheaval
travesty:	an unworthy, unrealistic imitation
unique:	unmatched, unequalled
validity:	soundness; truth

Index

INDEX

154

INDEX